The Canadian Real Estate Investing Blueprint

The Exact Strategies Canadians Have Used to Buy and Profit From Billions in Income Property

Authors:
Tom Karadza
Nick Karadza

ISBN: 9781793802354

I'd like to dedicate this book
to the great mentors that
have pushed me.

- Tom Karadza

I'd like to dedicate this book
to all the people who have
had a positive impact on my life.
Your guidance has been invaluable.

- Nick Karadza

Contents

Preface   viii

Introduction   ix

Part 1: Laying The Foundation   1

Chapter 1: How to Create a Life of Income in 29 Days or Less   2

Chapter 2: Quick Star #1: Preparation   16

Chapter 3: Quick Star #2: Systems   30

Chapter 4: Quick Star #3: Marketing   41

Chapter 5: Quick Star #4: Professionals   58

Chapter 6: The "Magic Snowball" That Keeps Your Portfolio Growing   79

Chapter 7: The Most Important Key to Success in Real Estate   84

Part 2: Beyond The Basics   93

Chapter 8: Sometimes Investing Can Be Boring   94

Chapter 9: Number Crunching For Single Rental Units   103

Chapter 10: 5 Things That Might Be Holding You Back   115

Chapter 11: Using Rock Star Marketing Systems to Fill Your Property – Part 1   126

Chapter 12: Using Rock Star Marketing Systems to Fill Your Property – Part 2   137

Chapter 13: Tips on Closing and Managing the Deal   145

Part 3: Student Rentals   157

Chapter 14: Back to School with Student Rentals   158

Chapter 15: Class #202 Advanced Student Rentals   166

Chapter 16: Attracting Students to Your Property   175

Part 4: Lease Options   188

Chapter 17: Lease Option Investing   189

Chapter 18: Lease Option Fundamentals   198

Chapter 19: How to Rent Your Home Fast & for Top Dollar   208

Chapter 20: Mastering Online Exposure & Call Backs   215

Chapter 21: Walking Possible Tenants Through Their Option   224

Chapter 22: The Key Ingredients for Selecting Lease/Option Tenants   235

Chapter 23: How to Profit Big Time from People Who Hate Your Property   248

Part 5: Negotiation & Persuasion   256

Chapter 24: The Offer & Negotiation Tips   257

Chapter 25: The Science of Persuasion   264

Part 6: Advanced Lessons   270

Chapter 26: Property Management Tips Learned the Hard Way   271

Chapter 27: Advanced Tips: Managing for Maximum Cash Flow   280

Chapter 28: Housing Market Fundamentals   299

Chapter 29: Using Joint Venture Agreements to Purchase   308
Cash Flowing Real Estate

Chapter 30: Getting a Big Fat Cheque from Your Real   315
Estate Investments

Next Steps...   323

Preface

These pages tell it all. We don't hold back from sharing all of our investing secrets. We've offered this information in different forms at different times to the members we work with, but never in one easy, convenient location.

This book goes beyond the basics and gives you the step-by-step practical strategies to successfully invest in a wide range of investment properties. We get specific, share examples, numbers, and go in-depth to answers the best questions we get from investors.

If at any point you have questions about what you're reading or your investments reach out to us; we'd love to talk to you.

Email your questions to:

TomAndNick@rockstarinnercircle.com

Or tweet us @rockstar_re

Follow us on Instagram @rockstarinnercircle

Facebook: www.facebook.com/RockStarInnerCircle

Introduction

All of your dreams are 100% possible, that's the good news. But first, we want to start with the bad news. The bad news is that the destruction of the middle class in Canada is a real thing.

The gap between income levels in this country and asset prices, like real estate, continue to widen. The increasing pace of this divide will catch thousands of Canadians unprepared. They'll wake up one day wondering what happened. They'll ask why their pensions, if they're lucky to even have one, can barely pay for rent and why the value of their RRSPs hasn't gone up in real terms in decades.

They'll scratch their heads wondering if the debt taken on for University and College was worth the years of payments. They will ask why their careers haven't been able to create the lifestyle that they had envisioned for themselves and their families.

The reason for this is that most Canadians don't understand how the money system actually works and it's not something we teach in school. This missing information causes most Canadians to focus on the short-term, going to school and choosing a career, instead of planning for the long-term, buying or creating good, income producing, assets as soon as they can.

Here's the core issue. In Canada, our money system is operated by the Bank of Canada. The Bank of Canada has a goal, as stated on their website, to ensure the cost of living in the country will increase at a rate of 2% annually. That sounds more than reasonable doesn't it? The problem lies in the execution. Unfortunately, they don't do a very good job of ensuring the prices of all things rise at 2% a year. Some things do, and some things don't.

For example, incomes tend to rise much closer to the 2% rate than do things like real estate. If your income rises 2% a year, every year, then your salary will double every 35 years. However, if real estate prices increase just a little bit higher, let's say 4% a year, then property prices will double every 18 years. If your income goes up at 2% a year and property prices go up 4% a year, then In the time it took for your income to double, property prices quadrupled.

If property prices increase 6% a year, then they double every 12 years. How can Canadians afford to own assets like real estate when their incomes levels are not keeping pace with the price of assets? And if you don't own any assets then each year this gap between incomes and assets grows, and it becomes more difficult for you to get into the game.

Quick aside: If you'd like to see a graphical chart of incomes versus real estate prices we've pulled out the Stats Canada and Toronto Real Estate Board prices and mapped them against each other, you can get a copy of that report at nomoremiddle.com.

Unless you're in an industry with rapidly growing income levels, it's extremely difficult to keep up with the cost of living, and our education system isn't helping us. Please don't misunderstand; we're not saying that education and going to university or college isn't important. We just believe that we need to explain to our younger generations that selecting a career isn't the "end point" of their journey into adulthood and financial independence. It's merely the beginning.

A good education and then picking up valuable skills in the workplace are the foundation which you can then use to buy or create your own asset base. If you cherish financial independence and freedom in your life, then to bet solely on your income as the vehicle to deliver that is a losing strategy. But if you work hard at your career, learn as much as possible, save up and then buy or create assets, the world is yours!

And this brings us back to the good news. Simply understanding the importance of personally owning good assets is half the battle.

The reason we believe in this approach of owning assets so much is that we're living proof of it what it can offer all of us. We both went to university and college, got good jobs in the software industry and picked up some extremely valuable skills. We then started flipping real estate and buying rental properties; we were beginning to build our own foundation of good assets.

Next, we went on to quit our jobs right in the middle of the growth trajectory of our careers and created a business around real estate that would help investors buy assets. That was the birth of Rock Star Real Estate, a brokerage based out of Oakville, Ontario that has now worked with thousands of Canadians on over a billion dollars worth of investment property. It's been featured on Profit Magazine's

Growth 500 list as one of the fastest growing companies in Canada for several years in a row.

Over the last ten years, we've seen countless Canadians change their financial futures with real estate. They've done it with single-family home rental properties, condo investments, student rentals, smaller multi-unit properties and larger apartment buildings. They've mastered the marketing of their properties, dealt with all the financing hurdles we all end up facing and handled all the unexpected curve balls that owning real estate will present. You can visit www.RockStarInnerCircle.com to learn more about their stories.

In this book, we condensed some of the most valuable lessons, used examples to illustrate them and tried our very best to make this information as easily digestible as possible. We have specifically chosen the strategies that we've personally seen the most Canadians use successfully.

We believe that by buying and owning assets like good income producing properties, we can take the rules of the money game as outlined by our Bank of Canada, turn them on their head, and make them work for us instead of against us. We can create cash flow, build equity, perhaps even earn some good appreciation and even build a lasting family legacy. And most importantly, as the destruction of the middle class continues we can ensure we're financially protecting ourselves.

Since we quit our jobs, we've been able to take six weeks, or more, of vacation every year. We've bought a coastal property on the Adriatic Sea in Croatia for family vacations, we travel to different spots in Europe every year, take amazing Caribbean vacations, we've bought and renovated amazing homes for our families, and it's all because of the power of real estate. We feel blessed and very grateful for the financial freedom we have.

Canada is a great country. A land full of opportunity for each of us. If two children of immigrant parents can live life on their terms in this country then so can you.

We hope that within the pages of this book you pick up one lesson, one idea or a single piece of motivation that will propel you to heights you never dreamed of.

Tom & Nick
Your Life. Your Terms.

Part 1:

Laying The Foundation

Chapter 1

How to Create a Lifetime of Income
In 29 Days or Less

In this first chapter, we're going to explain the concept of an "asset base," give you a start-up checklist and provide you with a schedule of activities to complete. This is what we call laying the foundation.

Sidebar: If you're an "experienced" real estate investor, then you'll be able to increase your profits and maximize your time from the information you're about to learn. If you're a "beginner" real estate investor, then Part 1 of this book will thoroughly explain how to get each of these preliminary steps completed.

OK, let's get a big point out of the way right up front. We've worked with a lot of investors. Young and old. All shapes and sizes. So, we know a little bit about "why" you are investing.

You're likely looking to:

> **A.** Create *financial freedom* so that you can have personal freedom.

OR

B. *Retire* from what you're doing so that you can live the life you really want.

OR

C. Create a *"little extra"* income in your life to supplement what you're already doing.

And it's right at this point where most people get things very wrong. They end up starting by chasing "deals" instead of "building assets."

Here's something you should tape to your bathroom mirror and commit to memory right now:

"Without your money working for you, you will never be able to stop working for money."

Most beginners, instead of looking to accumulate assets and have those assets spin off income, chase endless amounts of opportunities or lucrative deals (we like to call them "shiny objects") and end up with nothing.

Please re-read the above sentence again. Let it sink in.

And the media doesn't help much. With so many "fun" TV shows about "flipping" real estate for "quick cash" it's easy to lose focus.

Your Mission: Do not get distracted

Your job, as you go through this book, is to learn the best ways to build or expand an asset base and then focus your efforts like a laser beam.

Make a decision right now that you're willing to build yourself a base of assets that produce income.

Look around at any person who you believe has financial freedom. They have some assets somewhere that produce income. And very likely those assets are in one of two forms. They either have:

1) A Business

Some sort of business that puts money in their pockets on a regular basis. It produces cash flow.

2) A Portfolio of Real Estate

A group of properties that puts money in their pockets on a regular basis. It produces cash flow.

Now we're here to talk about real estate, so we'll stick to that topic, but as you'll learn, owning real estate is like running a business.

We'd like to share a story to really make this sink in because it's critical to you achieving the results you want.

We personally know several very successful income earners. They live in the Greater Toronto Area in Ontario, Canada and earn upwards of $300,000/year.

Recently, one of them lost his job due to consolidation in the industry they work in. That person had to scramble to find another source of income. He had two houses, several luxury cars, and their family was used to 5-star exotic vacations.

But without an immediate replacement to that person's income, he was going to have some serious financial difficulty. Quickly.

He had no asset base that made money for him, so he had to continue working for money.

Let's continue the story...

We know another person in the exact same industry who took his earnings and began buying and selling real estate. He made a lot of money doing it.

Big money. Bags of it.

He got really good at buying homes and then selling them for a quick profit.

That money went into buying bigger homes, more cars, and 5-star vacations. Sound familiar?

Then his company also got "downsized," and he had to scramble to find a new job to replace his income.

So, although he was good at flipping properties ("flipping" is real estate talk for buying properties and then selling them quickly) when his job disappeared, he couldn't flip more property because the banks wanted "proof of employment" before they would give him another mortgage.

He had no asset base that made money for him, so he had to continue working for money.

Again, the story continues...

The person who was flipping real estate had a lot of his friends get interested in how he was making so much money. Everyone was eager to copy his success.

They all wanted to make $100,000+ "flipping" real estate overnight. So, they chased what looked like good opportunities all over town.

Some of them made some money. Some of them lost some money.

But because "flipping" real estate is much more like **earning an income** than it is **producing an asset** for yourself they all had to continue working.

They had no asset base that made money for them, so they had to continue working for money.

Think about it.

Finding properties for a good deal, fixing them up, and then selling them produces an **income**.

You're not creating a group of assets that spin off cash flow.

It's much more like a job than anything else.

You have to keep finding properties, keep fixing them up and keep selling them to make money.

The moment you stop, the money stops.

We don't want that. And likely, you don't want that.

We want the money to never stop!

Buy & Hold Real Estate

Now there's a simple way to add income and build wealth to your life at the same time. And you can do it with real estate.

It's a strategy that you've heard before: Buy & Hold (and profit!)

If you're looking to live life on your terms, then you want an asset base that produces cash flow for you.

Owning positive cash flowing real estate = the asset base that you want to own.

And this is where we come in.

Buy & Hold real estate is buying real estate and holding it for a long period of time. There are many tips and tricks to maximize this strategy that we'll be going over during this book.

And before we continue, let's make something very clear.

Anyone can buy a piece of real estate that generates negative cash flow (the revenue that the property generates does not cover the expenses: mortgage, property taxes, insurance, etc.).

But not you.

You are acquiring positive cash flow real estate because in good economic times, or poor economic times positive cash flow real estate is easy to hold onto. We're speaking from experience here and will share more in future lessons.

Startup Checklist: The Four Pillars of Creating a Real Estate Empire

There are four "pillars" of a successful real estate asset base that generates consistent positive cash flow. Each of these is a necessary component in starting or expanding your real estate empire... They are, in essence, <u>your foundation</u>.

1. **Preparation:** In the preparation stage you will make important decisions about your real estate portfolio: areas you will invest in, the types of properties that you'll focus on, and the financing that you'll secure.

2. **Systems:** In the systems stage you'll structure the steps you will use to find properties and fill properties. Without proven repeatable systems that you can turn on and off like a light switch, your <u>business</u> is more like a <u>hobby</u>.

3. **Marketing:** In the marketing stage you will create your advertisements and learn the psychology behind making them magnetic – attracting tenants to you, day in and day out.

4. **Professionals:** In the professionals stage you will understand why not all professionals are created equal. There are specific reasons why you'll need multiple lawyer contacts, and specific things to look for in your accountant.

As we've mentioned, we'll cover each of these in-depth over the next four chapters. For now, let's identify some core action steps to complete in successfully building a real estate asset base.

Eight Steps to Acquiring Your First or Next Cash Flow Producing Asset

<u>Note</u>: These eight steps are organized in chronological order for your convenience.

✓ <u>DEVISE</u> your plan. (Activity Time: 3 Days) Every house has a set of blueprints used to build it. Your asset base should have one too.

Do you want a little extra income or are you building the next great real estate empire?

Do you want one property this year, or ten?

And why are you doing this? A big reason "why" helps you push through the days that you feel like sitting on the couch watching reality TV instead of marching towards your finish line.

✓ <u>DECIDE</u> on an area. (Activity Time: 5 Days) Not all markets are created equal. Factors that determine a good place to invest include: growing population, diverse employment, higher than average family income levels, infrastructure and transportation improvements. A good place to look for this information is the local city Economic Development office and/or City Planner. Also, Statistics Canada has fantastic resources for this: (www.StatCan.gc.ca)

✓ <u>DEFINE</u> the properties. (Activity Time: 2 Days) Which types of properties will you focus on? Single-family homes? Duplexes and triplexes? Student rentals? Pre-construction? Condos? Multi-unit apartment buildings? Land? Office buildings? Strip malls? Public storage?

Remember to think about cash flow and how easy your

exit plan will be for each type. You will want your realtor to begin screening and sending you properties.

✓ <u>DESIGNATE</u> your professionals. (Activity Time: 4 Days) We personally use a mortgage broker who has had previous experience with investors and investor mortgages. The same applies to realtors. Our lawyer is a real estate specialist, and so is our accountant.

Having professionals who understand the real estate business can save you thousands of dollars in potential problems that they steer you away from. Spend the time to make some good choices and if possible never have one option to go to. Have a backup contact for each position.

✓ <u>DETERMINE</u> your financing. (Activity Time: 5 Days) What loan/mortgage programs do you qualify for? Do you know which ones apply to investors? Mortgage programs change monthly, and different programs serve different purposes.

✓ <u>DEVELOP</u> your system. (Activity Time: 6 Days) There are two main steps in a good real estate system. Screening for properties and filling the properties with tenants.

First, you'll want to create a list of "features" that your property must have (for example: 3 bedrooms, 2 bathrooms, family neighbourhood, etc.). Second, you'll want to create a marketing system that attracts people to your property like clockwork.

✓ <u>DEVOTE</u> yourself to marketing. (Activity Time: 2 Days) Become familiar with the local newspapers: the costs, the delivery schedules, discounts for ads running longer than 7 days. Begin collecting online advertising websites. We personally use Kijiji.ca and GottaRent.com frequently.

✓ DESIGN your offer. (Activity Time: 1 Day) A good offer has 2-3 critical components. First, a clause allowing you enough time to secure financing. Second, a clause allowing you to have a professional home inspection. Both of those should allow you to walk away if the results are "not suitable" for you for any reason. Third, a price. You will want recently sold comparables to make this decision, not listing prices – sold prices.

Based on the "Activity Time" allotted for each of these activities, it should take you no more than 29 days.

29 days and you can secure an asset
that produces a lifetime of income!

And, truthfully, we've seen it happen much faster, even for a first-time investor. They had the right plan and took action on it … and so can you!

Now let's circle back briefly to this idea of Buy & Hold real estate.

You may have noticed that earlier we added: "and Profit!" to the end of Buy & Hold.

For simplicity sake, when we say Buy & Hold, let's use a single-family home that a tenant rents out. We'll cover all sorts of different examples in the lessons ahead.

At first, this strategy may not generate life-changing income for you, but the long-term wealth building opportunity is absolutely incredible.

Let's take a look at a typical home that we come across. The purchase price is $390,000. That's around the average price of a starter home in several communities within an hour's drive of the Greater Toronto Area (our neck of the woods).

This home has three bedrooms and 2 bathrooms. It could be a single-family home or a townhome.

To invest in this home, you go to the bank and get an investor mortgage requiring you to have a 20% down payment.

Let's review the numbers with this investment:

Names:	Numbers:	Notes:
Purchase Price	$390,000	
Down Payment	$78,000	20% Down
Mortgage Loan	$312,000	Investment Mortgage
Monthly Mortgage Payment	$1,460	
Monthly Property Taxes	$300	2.9% Interest Rate &
Monthly Property Insurance	$70	25 Year Amortization
Total Monthly Payment	$1,830	
Monthly Rental Income	$1,950	
Monthly Positive Cash Flow	$120	

Based on this example, you would be earning $120 each and every month from this single-family home. That doesn't get you jumping up and down with excitement, does it?

But that's not the whole story...

Note: A change in interest rates could make a significant impact on your monthly cash flow. We used 2.9% for the purpose of this example, but you will need to make your calculations based on your rate.

Let's take a closer look because this single-family home is really an incredible wealth building machine.

Here are your four income streams:

1. **Monthly Positive Cash Flow:** In the example, you would be earning $120 each month from this investment. You can take that and live your Rock Star Life! OK, maybe not yet, but soon!

2. **Mortgage Loan Reduction:** Each month you are building equity into your investment. This is very different from most other types of investing. What we mean is that each month that the tenant pays you rent, you send a mortgage payment to the bank. A portion of this payment is reducing the mortgage balance every single month. And every dollar that is paid off the mortgage is wealth to you. You have your tenant paying off your debt – how great is that? In this example, it works out to be $742/month. That's a second income stream to you.

3. **Appreciation:** Over time your property will appreciate. Even if your property only appreciates at 3% a year, it would be worth $401,700 after the first year you owned it. That's an extra $11,700 a year and is another income stream for you. If you divide $11,700 by 12 months, it equals $975 each month.

4. **Tax Savings:** At the end of the year, for tax purposes, your property will show a loss. You are allowed to depreciate your property, and this is an expense that you don't have to pay for. Also, your property and mortgage insurance are expenses. These will likely create a tax loss, which you can use to reduce the amount of taxes you pay at the end of the year. If we're

conservative and assume this saves you $1,000 at the end of the year, it would equal $83 each month.

Are your wheels turning with excitement yet? They should be!

Now, one single family home provides you with these four income streams. Let's add them up:

> Monthly Positive Cash Flow: $120
> Monthly Loan Reduction: $742
> Monthly Appreciation: $975
> Monthly Tax Savings: $83

> **Total Monthly Return: $1,920**

Pretty neat, eh? And this is just from **one** home. What happens if you own two or three? Do the math. These numbers get large very quickly.

But the hidden factor in all of this is that most of the $1,920 is hidden. You can't spend it. So, you can't book that trip to Tuscany or that surfing adventure to Costa Rica.

Real estate investing is powerful because it automatically forces you to build your wealth.

In terms of wealth building assets, it really doesn't get any better than this.

This is an "overview" chapter.

It is intentional. This was by design. We've arranged it this way so experienced folks can get started immediately, and beginners can get a general idea of what we'll be covering in Part 1.

Now, on to our assignments...

Chapter 1's Assignment

1) If you are an "experienced" investor, **get started immediately** by following the Startup Checklist and Eight Steps. You should be able to get moving quickly.

2) If you are a "beginning" student, **begin brainstorming ideas**: possible plans for your real estate empire, reasons why you are doing this, communities that you know fit some of the criteria we've discussed. We'll provide you with plenty of options over the next couple of chapters, but we'd like you to begin brainstorming for yourself at this point.

Chapter 2

Quick Start #1: Preparation

In order to build a successful real estate asset base that produces cash flow, there are several key decisions you need to make. In this chapter, we'll examine them as we look at the first of the **"Four Pillars of a Cash Flow Generating Real Estate Portfolio."**

Pillar #1: Preparation

There's an old adage that says, *"Fail to plan, plan to fail"* and there is truth to that. We've all heard of that "lucky" person who strikes it rich, but for the most part, it takes a solid plan of action to make things work.

So, let's make some decisions regarding your real estate investing.

Sidebar: Through this book, we'll be sharing a lot of "ideas" to help explain the lessons in each chapter. We're idea machines! We can look at a strategy or tactic and think of dozens of ideas for using it. We're not saying this to brag; it's just the way we are. The point that we're trying to make is that it's important you read each and every chapter even if you think you "know it" already … We're bound to share some variations that you've never thought of before, which could equal a BIG cash flow or profit increase for you.

There are three key elements of forming the foundation of your real estate portfolio that we want to mention. We call them **Rock Star TNT™**, and if you get these three things right, you're setting yourself up for explosive growth.

Rock Star TNT™

T – Target Areas
N – Niche Properties
T – Types of Financing

These are the three things that you'll want to determine in this chapter as we get the blueprint for your real estate portfolio set.

And as we make our way through them, we'll be sharing some "real life" case study examples to get you thinking about what to do with your own investing.

We'll even be sharing some of our own personal "untapped" ideas that we plan on using in the future.

```
Rock Star TNT™
T= Target Areas
```

Note: We will use terms like "target areas" and "communities" interchangeably.

We tell all of our own private Inner Circle coaching members that there are 4 primary criteria that we look at in deciding what target area we want to invest in... These are the fundamentals:

1. A community that has growing demand.

A famous marketer once said that even he could run a successful restaurant if he had a starving crowd waiting outside. And that is what you're looking for. You want to invest in communities where a "starving crowd" already exists.

The most obvious examples of this in real estate are student rental properties. You literally have a starving crowd of students who are looking for a house to rent close to a university or college. Student rentals have pros and cons, which we will cover in Part 3. For now, we want to learn how to find areas where starving crowds exist on a whole.

2. A community that has a higher than average income.

People who are spending money in a community will drive up the value of real estate. And a community with growing income levels has "staying power." It usually means there are jobs directly in the area, or in close proximity and it often means there is diverse employment.

You want to make your investments as simple as possible, and an area with multiple sources of employment creates a healthy and active real estate market. It provides a good base of tenants, first-time buyers and "move up" buyers.

3. A community with new transportation or infrastructure projects.

It's proven that new transportation routes will increase the demand for nearby real estate. You don't have to be a rocket scientist to figure that out. Just look back to your own childhood.

As kids growing up we can recall when a brand-new highway that was built right through Mississauga (a bedroom community on the west side of Toronto). We rode our bikes on it before it was finished. At that time, there were only farmers' fields on either side of that highway. Today, you can't fit another development anywhere close to it. Every square kilometre has been developed. And new infrastructure projects don't only mean transportation developments. They can include things like water and sewage access.

For example, Milton, Ontario, was a sleepy town for years. There was almost zero development even though they sat next to a rapidly growing urban community. The reason? They had no way to expand their current sewage system. Once a new "big pipe" was built to handle extra demand, there was an explosion of new development. If you had purchased a property in that community at the beginning of that wave, you would have earned consistent amounts of increased equity almost monthly for over 3 years.

There are many "target areas" for you to choose from. And as long as you remember to focus on **growing demand** (population), **higher than average income** (diverse employment), and **new transportation and infrastructure projects** you are setting yourself up for success.

Enough theory though, you are a Rock Star, right? We want you to gain direct knowledge of how to gather this information.

Let's walk through these steps together and we'll show you exactly what we do ourselves to find this data...

Step #1: Learn How to Use Existing Tools at Your Fingertips

Statistics Canada (www.statcan.gc.ca) does a fantastic job of compiling data, there's not much for you to do. Once you figure out how to use the tools on its website, you'll be hooked.

It's the most complete compilation of data that we've found. And the best part, it's free. Well, we actually all pay for this via taxes but that doesn't change the fact that this is the most **overlooked and underestimated** source of real estate investing data.

Let's show you why.

Remember, as investors we want to invest in areas with increasing demand (population) and above average income.

Well, the Statistics Canada website provides us with "Community Profiles" that detail this information for us.

Now stick with us, because this is where things get really exciting. Using the tools available to you on this page, you can quickly analyze your target investment areas by comparing them to the provincial averages.

The report will show you the **Population** change in your targeted area. And it gets better. If you scroll down the page you'll find the **Income Data** that we're looking for:

So, looking at the community profile for the Kitchener-Cambridge-Waterloo are, we can clearly see for ourselves that this area, Ontario has a growing population and income levels that are above the provincial averages.

Note: You can find the latest stats on the government website.

How do you interpret this data?

We don't need population growth numbers to exceed the provincial average because sometimes communities grow for reasons that don't sustain an active real estate market.

For example, retirement communities and vacation communities can have population growth above provincial averages but no growth in income. So, population growth alone can be a false indicator.

What we do want to see is population growth AND income levels above the provincial average. Together they're a powerful force. In this particular example, we get both. The Kitchener area has a population growth of 8.9% AND income levels above the provincial average.

Bottom Line: Population growth needs to exist but doesn't need to exceed the provincial average. Income levels should be above the provincial average. Together they ensure an active economy and set a solid foundation for your real estate portfolio.

These charts can be used to analyze cities right across Canada. Everywhere from Vancouver, British Columbia to St. John's, Newfoundland.

Step #2: Get familiar with transportation and infrastructure developments for the province you're looking to invest in.

A quick Google search for "Alberta infrastructure projects" or "British Columbia Transportation and Infrastructure" or "Ontario transportations developments" will turn up good sources of information.

These are excellent sources of information for upcoming infrastructure projects. And the best single source for the very latest developments is Google News.

The information is out there. You just need to know where to look for it.

Remember, there's a big difference between a government "announcement" and shovels actually hitting the ground. It often takes years for projects to get started, sometimes decades. Need a good example?

The Red Hill Valley Expressway in Hamilton – the origins of that project can be traced back to the 1950s, but the project didn't actually start until 2004 and didn't open until 2007, more than 50 years after being proposed.

Don't want to spend time searching for new information? No problem. You can set up News Alerts so anytime something matching your criteria hits Google News it will be emailed to you.

```
Rock Star TNT™
N = Niche Properties
```

There is no money in becoming a **generalist**. Neurosurgeons make big money because they are specialists. Specialization = Profits. You need to become a **property specialist.**

There are a series of property types you need to be aware of. And you'll want to become an expert in **one or two** of these property types. Any more and you're likely stretching yourself too thin.

As we cover each property type, you should be asking yourself these three questions:

1) How can I find properties like this?
2) How can I finance properties like this?
3) How can I profit from properties like this?
4) What is my exit strategy for properties like this?
5) Where are the hidden costs for properties like this?

1. Single Family Homes: Think of "little green houses" in the Monopoly® board game. They can make for a solid asset base of cash flowing real estate. And they are plentiful; single-family homes are the cornerstone of communities across Canada. They can be financed easily and sold relatively quickly in almost any market. The challenges? They can be tricky to make cash flow, especially in higher-priced urban markets like Vancouver, Calgary and Toronto. We will cover specific strategies and tactics to illustrate how profitable these can be in future chapters.

2. Student Rental Properties: Often you can have five to nine students in a house paying anywhere from $300 to $650 a month, each! As a result, these properties cash flow extremely well. Maintenance will be slightly higher than on a single-family home, and you have to be aware of proper insurance requirements, but a constant supply of hungry tenants (literally!) can offset these other challenges.

3. Duplexes & Triplexes: A great way to increase the cash flow of any property is to maximize the revenue. A single building that can be set up to house two or three families has been a classic real estate investment for decades. There are benefits of having "one roof" and three families in a single-family property. The primary advantage – diversified income – if one family leaves, you have two others paying rent. The chief challenge – often many of these properties are "non-conforming" and don't meet local by-law standards for things like utility meters, entrances/exits, and parking.

4. Small Multi-Unit Apartments: A six-plex or an eight-plex is a small building with no elevators and above ground parking. These are typically valued by the income generated and are often too small for full-time property management. You will likely have to manage this type of property yourself. They can be excellent investments, and because commercial financing can be secured for these (because they are six units and above) financing can be obtained based on the building's capitalization rate instead of your personal debt service ratios.

5. Large Multi-Unit Apartments: Think of six-storey buildings or higher with ten or more units per floor. These buildings are large enough to have dedicated property management and often an "on-site superintendent" to handle the day-to-day business activities. Financing is obtained by the buildings financials and your down payment. This is considered a commercial property and is one of the few categories of commercial real estate that CMHC will ensure up to 85% loan to value. With a 15% down payment, you can purchase this type of property. Hidden costs? Large expenses like underground garage repairs or balcony updating. This is considered one of the safest and most conservative commercial real estate investments.

6. Strip Malls: Think of a mall with a Tim Horton's on the corner, a grocery store as the anchor tenant, and a series of convenience stores, clothing stores, nail salons, and family doctor's offices. With stable tenants, these can provide years of uninterrupted cash flow. However, many of these malls are comprised of small businesses with unproven business models. As a result, banks require large down payments, usually 35% or much higher, and even with a Grade-A business like Tim Hortons as one of the tenants, financing can be difficult to secure unless you have deep pockets and a proven track record.

7. Office Buildings: Similar to strip malls, these typically belong to large real estate holding companies. To build from scratch requires local city zoning approvals and anchor tenants committed to long-term leases. Financing is difficult to obtain without a proven business plan backed by a strong balance sheet.

8. Industrial Property: Warehouse space can be a lucrative investment. A single tenant may rent out a large warehouse and only use a portion of the space, greatly reducing the wear and tear on the property. Often industrial space sits on land that can be sub-divided and used to build more buildings.

The challenges – often the city may sell land for industrial use with assurances that future buildings are erected on the land. If you can't deliver on promises to further develop the property you may be forced into a difficult financial situation. And because large industrial properties may have only one tenant, if they leave you may have to carry the property vacant through a tough economic cycle.

9. Land: Some of the largest fortunes have been by purchasing land. You need to have deep pockets and staying power but the payoffs can be huge. Large tracts of land are often purchased by investors well in front of urban sprawl. As development approaches, pieces of land are sold off for residential subdivisions and commercial office parks.

As you can tell, there is a **wide range** of real estate opportunities available, ranging from $400,000 single family homes to $18,000,000 multi-unit apartment complexes.

Within these property types, there are opportunities for massive amounts of cash flow and profits, which is exactly why real estate investing can get so exciting and so distracting!

Recommendation: Unless there is a reason to do otherwise, focus your efforts on one or two of these property niches. We're repeating this because real estate investors tend to get distracted easily. And if there's any advice we would like to share, it's this:

The "real money" in real estate comes from building an asset base of cash flowing real estate. It doesn't come from chasing "deals."

Focus on building a real asset base instead of chasing income. We can't say it enough. We've spent a lot of time ourselves chasing deals with very little to show for it. Our real wealth and money have come from building a base of properties one brick at a time.

To be perfectly honest, we didn't realize the power of an asset base until we had built the beginnings of our own. At that point, a "magical snowball" begins to build where cash flow combined with equity build-up and appreciation begin to multiply your wealth building efforts.

> Rock Star TNT™
> **T = Types of Financing**

The final key factor from our first Pillar (Preparation) is to determine what financing options you will focus on.

There are 2 basic types of financing:

a. Conventional
b. High Ratio

Conventional Financing: This is where the bank is directly lending to you with no "mortgage insurance" required for your purchase. For residential properties (typically, properties with less than six units) conventional financing is used any time a down payment of 20% or more is used. With commercial properties, conventional financing requires a 30% down payment or more depending on the property type.

High Ratio Financing: Any purchase with a down payment less than 20%. This is the most commonly used financing type for beginner investors. Typically, as a beginner, you are looking to acquire real estate with as little money down as possible. And who can blame that approach? Less money down usually increases your Return on Investment. However, it can reduce your cash flow because your mortgage amount is greater than with conventional financing. Also, there will be a mortgage insurance fee placed onto the balance of your mortgage on the closing day. And, depending on your income level, you may be quickly reaching a limit to the number of properties you can purchase with high ratio financing.

Note: The Canadian Housing & Mortgage Corporation (CMHC) has eliminated its high ratio financing in an effort to cool the housing market. You'll want to reach out to a good mortgage broker to learn about plans with other insurers.

Overall, we are fans of using high ratio mortgages when done with the right tactics and on the right properties.

For example, a good candidate would be a property that produces positive cash flow and that you plan on holding for several years. If you are looking to sell the property quickly it may be difficult to force the appreciation of the property high enough to sell for a profit after your mortgage insurance fee has been accounted for.

Note: By positive cash flow, we mean an investment property where after the mortgage, property taxes, and insurance payments are made, there is money left over for your bank account every month.

Mortgage insurance rates will range anywhere from 2% to 3.5% depending on:

1) Property Type (single family versus multi-unit apartment)
2) Amortization (15 year versus 25 year)

3) Down Payment (5% versus 10% versus 15%)

An easy way to begin determining your financing is to decide which type of property you will begin to specialize in. We're going to cover how to deal with and what to look for in mortgage brokers in Chapter 4 and explain what to ask them so that you can map out your own plan.

Chapter 2's Assignments

1) For experienced investors with existing properties, visit the Community Profiles on Statistics Canada's website and evaluate your current investments.

2) For beginners start evaluating areas within a 90-minute drive of where you live. Look for increasing population and higher than average income levels. Having an understanding of this data will make your investing decisions very simple. And you'll be able to sleep easy knowing that you're investing with "the fundamentals" on your side. You are tipping the odds in your favour following this process, and you will have a massive advantage over other investors who are discounting or ignoring this data.

Chapter 3

As we mentioned in Chapter 2, having a profitable real estate portfolio involves **"Four Pillars."** In the last chapter, we examined Pillar #1, which was Preparation. In Chapter 3 we'll be examining the second of the **"Four Pillars of a Cash Flow Generating Real Estate Portfolio."**

<u>Pillar #2: Systems</u>

We're going to begin setting up the systems of your real estate business. Over the past several years we've been fortunate to work directly with many investors. And this experience has proven to be very valuable to us.

Many people believe they don't have what it takes to be a real estate investor. They don't have the "know how" or the "courage" to deal with the perceived "issues" that arise.

However, watching literally more than 100 beginner investors over the past 36 months has shown us that, time after time, you can achieve success in real estate with some key ingredients.

Let us explain...

Michael E. Gerber wrote a fantastic book, *The E-Myth*, which summarizes our findings beautifully. He explains that there is an "Entrepreneurial Myth" in existence. And that myth is the idea that anyone can go from nothing to running their own business.

For example, the greatest home-based wedding cake baker in town decides that she would like to open up their own retail store. And she mistakenly believes that because she is a master cake baker, she can **build a business.**

We've learned from direct experience in both our real estate investing business and running our own brokerage that there is a **big difference** between "knowing how to do the work" and "building a business."

And your real estate investment portfolio is very much like running an active business. And you must treat it like one. It's not enough to say, "I am a real estate investor" and then buy a property.

Before you throw yourself full force into building your real estate portfolio, you must understand that you are starting down the path of running an "active business."

Anyone who claims that real estate investing generates purely "passive income" is not sharing the whole story. You can make it feel "passive," and that requires the use of business systems.

Real Estate Investing = An Active Business

We regularly meet all walks of people who "know they should get started" but aren't sure where to begin.

We've boiled down why people feel this way to two reasons:

1. **Commitment.**
2. **Systems.**

If you're looking to grow a sizeable real estate portfolio, you must ask yourself, "Are you up to it?"

And it's a difficult question to answer because you don't know what you have to be "up to." Real estate has many twists and turns, so it's almost impossible to define.

So, the better question is, are you able to completely commit yourself to building an asset base that will produce ongoing income for yourself and leave a legacy on your behalf for years to come?

If your answer is yes, and you're willing to trust the process (because real estate investing, like anything else, is a process), you are halfway home!

You need to trust that this journey will be a growing experience that, when done properly, will build a beautiful basket of golden eggs that will produce income for life.

Once you've made this commitment, the next parts are laying down the systems that will get you there, and having the discipline to follow them.

The Two Primary Systems You Must Develop

The two primary real estate business systems that you want to develop are:

A) **Property Acquisition** - finding and acquiring properties that meet your criteria and fit your goals.

B) **Marketing** – a proven process to follow that generate "tenant leads" (also known as "potential customers") for your business.

Most people complicate matters when they shouldn't. Creating a real estate portfolio is rather simple when you follow a system.

Most of the tasks required for each are straightforward. Let's cover them together step-by-step.

Property Acquisition

You want to get very clear on the type or types of property you want to specialize in. It's not good enough to call yourself a "real estate investor." You want to become a specialist. In Chapter 2, we covered that specialists are paid more than generalists.

Remember our example of heart surgeons being paid more than general family practitioners? So, you want to become a real estate specialist. Pick your property categories and become super knowledgeable about them.

The key to this is select appropriate properties for your goals. There are some characteristics of investing that we want to quickly mention:

Consider residential properties, both single family and multi-unit apartment buildings. There are a gazillion different types of real estate investments, many of which we covered together in Chapter 2, but the primary ones are broken into two categories: residential and commercial.

The primary reasons for focusing on residential properties, at least initially, are: they are the easiest properties to find, they are the easiest to finance, they are the easiest to market, and they are the easiest to get professional help with.

<u>Step One</u>: Finding Your Properties

In Chapter 2, we covered picking a "fundamentally correct" area to invest in. We focused on population trends, income levels, and infrastructure developments.

Once you have your area, you want to develop a standard process and criteria for finding homes.

For example, if you've decided to focus on residential properties you can use existing tools like www.Realtor.ca that aggregate listings across Canada for anything that is six units or less.

For residential multi-unit buildings greater than four units, you can also use www.Realtor.ca for your search. Instead of choosing the "Residential Properties", you would select "Commercial Properties."

Many investors mistakenly believe there is one system for all listed real estate properties. You should understand that real estate across Canada is organized into "Real Estate Boards." For example, The Kitchener Waterloo Real Estate Board or the Winnipeg Real Estate Board.

Properties are "listed" for sale on the local real estate board, and that data is shared with www.Realtor.ca with a delay of about 48 hours or so.

This means that you'll also want to develop a relationship with a local realtor. Explain your goals and your criteria and have them email you a list of newly listed properties as they become available. Their real estate boards allow them to set up this type of notification for you without much hassle.

Here's A Big Tip for You

Many people know that when looking at single-family homes, we believe in the "starter home category." This is the category of homes that always has the most interest, from renters and buyers. And we like to make sure all our investments are "in demand," so this category is the perfect place to invest into.

In good economic times, or poor economic times, "starter homes" are always in demand. Housing is a "need" after all. Not a "want." That's a big reason we're not believers of investing in high-end real estate - at least not yet. You may want to stick to "bread and butter" style homes as well.

But we take this one step further and put a little twist on it:

We've found that if you focus on the higher end of the starter home category, you attract better tenants.

Let's use our example city of Kitchener, Ontario. You can buy a "starter" townhome for $300,000. It's older, needs some work, and isn't in a nice complex. But it qualifies as a "starter" home. However, if you acquire the "higher end" starter home, then you appeal to people's emotions. Most people have a dream of living in their own home, and the higher end of the starter home category appeals to that. So instead of buying a $300,000 townhome because that's the cheapest property in the category, we usually acquire a $400,000 single family home.

This does a few things:

- **It separates us from other investors.** Most investors want the cheapest property available. As a result, there is often more competition for tenants in that category. With our property, there is less competition because there are fewer investors spending slightly more on a nicer piece of real estate.

- **We appeal to a tenant's emotions.** There's nothing too appealing about a run-down home. A nice property gets people excited. It makes the property easier to rent, and ultimately it attracts better tenants. As a result, we can charge more for the home, so the tenants need to be able to pay a higher rent. Good homes attract good tenants.

- **It strengthens our portfolio.** With a good mix of nice single-family homes in our portfolio, we have a strong asset base. They will rent out easily, and we have a very clear and defined exit plan. We can sell them without much hassle.

What About Multi-Unit Properties?

This idea applies to other forms of property as well. For example, it is widely accepted with experienced multi-unit real estate investors that a building full of "bachelor apartments" doesn't attract stable tenants.

Instead, a building full of "two-bedroom" apartments attracts a more stable tenant, and as a result, a more stable revenue stream. This type of building has moved up the "rent ladder" to attract better tenants. Banks and mortgage insurers are also more willing to lend on buildings with a good ratio of two-bedroom apartments in the building. That alone should be instructive when you're making your investment decisions.

Bottom line: Once you've selected the category of property you'll invest in – choose the higher end of the category. You'll reduce competition and stand out from the crowd.

Commercial properties (this includes multi-unit residential buildings over 6 units), are not always listed on the commercial area of www.Realtor.ca. In fact, it's estimated that only about 20% of them actually get listed in the regular fashion and find their way to www.Realtor.ca.

There is no "one place" to look for these buildings. They're often traded between commercial real estate brokerages and sold on an "exclusive" basis. This means that they're much harder to find – but it can be done and we'll be covering this in greater detail.

So…

As you build your system for finding properties you'll want to be on the lookout for niche commercial real estate brokerages that focus on your category of property.

Step Two: Financing Your Properties

Now, there are literally dozens and dozens of financing options available to you. So, what we want to give you are our personal recommendations. When you're planning your investments, you will want to plan ahead. Some investing options are good for two to three purchases but will be prohibitive after that.

When you're beginning, the best place to start is with a mortgage broker who works with investors. Make some phone calls and begin asking around. Meet with a few of them and outline your plan.

How will you know if they're competent enough to work with you?

Test them.

Ask them these questions:

1. How much volume in mortgage business do they do annually? (If they do more than $50 Million they're doing enough business to likely understand how to work with investors – from our experience anyway!)

2. What is their mortgage portfolio default ratio? (If it's really low – like under 0.4%, they likely have mortgage underwriters that really like them and are willing to work with them aggressively.)

Also, Get familiar with CMHC's Mortgage Insurance products available to real estate investors. Sometimes they have none and other times they have multiple.

For the latest stuff, you can poke around their website here: https://www.cmhc-schl.gc.ca/en/co/moloin/index.cfm

Most banks in Canada will not offer high ratio mortgages in Canada (less than 20% down) because they only work with CMHC as their mortgage insurer.

The other two companies that have "on-again-off-again" residential investment property mortgage products are www.Genworth.ca and www.CanadaGuaranty.ca.

The reason you'll want to work with a good mortgage broker instead of just with a bank is they'll likely have access to the mortgage products from Genworth and Canada Guaranty (the Canadian arm of AIG).

Just relying on your bank will limit your option.

Even if all of these mortgage insurers have nothing great going for investors at the time, you need them. A good mortgage broker will likely have access to private lenders or Mortgage Investment Corporations (MICs) that may be another source of funds for you.

Bottom Line: Spend the time to find a good, experienced mortgage broker. They may be your key to buying multiple properties.

What About Commercial Property Financing?

The most widely available mortgage products are available for multi-unit apartment buildings. Both CMHC and the major banks consider these properties to be the least risky type of commercial investments.

The reason? A stable source of revenue.

Strip malls, office buildings, and industrial space can have vacancies for months, even years at a time. Apartment buildings provide shelter, which as you know by now, is "a need."

It's a common myth that you must put down at least 25% to 35% to buy large multi-unit apartment buildings.

That is not the case.

They will loan up to 85% of the value of the building. There are things like application fees and structural inspections that you'll have to pay for.

Note: Down payments of 25% and higher are common for most other commercial real estate property types.

As you grow as an investor your **Finding** and **Financing** should become a smooth part of your property acquisition systems.

Chapter 3 Assignments

1) **Start searching.** Check out properties on www.Realtor.ca. Spend time on different property types so that you get familiar with how they are listed for sale.

2) **Get notified.** If you are focused on single-family homes, reach out to a couple of local realtors and get yourself on their email notification lists. If you are focused on commercial real estate, build your database of local commercial brokerages. Use Google.ca to track down two or three in your area and put yourself on their email notification lists.

3) **Understand mortgage products.** Spend 15 minutes reviewing CMHC's website. In a short while, you'll have a better understanding of investment mortgages than 95% of all bankers and brokers.

Chapter 4

Quick Start #3: Marketing

There's an acronym we've been using ourselves for years, and we want you to get very familiar with it because it's proven to be extremely profitable.

Here you go - > L-A-A-P:

L – <u>LEADS</u> for your properties
A – <u>APPOINTMENTS</u> for your properties
A – <u>APPLICATIONS</u> to rent or to buy your properties
P – <u>PROFIT</u> from your properties

Whenever you're working with a property, you should have a very clear starting point and a very clear finish.

Running a "LAAP" around your high school track has all of these things. Corny, we know, but profitable, very profitable!

Almost Everyone Lacks a Marketing System

Almost every single real estate investor we have ever met is lacking a marketing system. They get so caught up in the details that they misunderstand where the real value of their business comes from.

It doesn't come from the property itself.

Let us repeat that.

The value of your real estate business DOES NOT come from your properties.

Your properties produce a lot of profit for you, but they only do that if they are producing cash flow. And how do properties produce cash flow? By having tenants pay rent. Or, if you're "flipping" a property, the money comes from selling the property.

Let's illustrate with an example.

What is McDonald's main business advantage? Is it the quality of their hamburgers? Definitely not.

The value in the McDonald's business model comes from having a "system" that gets kids working for minimum wage to produce food quickly and reliably like clockwork.

You can make a better burger than McDonald's on your backyard BBQ.

But do you have a better system than McDonald's for producing thousands of burgers a day?

Let's use a real estate example to drive this point home...

"REAL ESTATE: Forcing Equity Appreciation"
Many real estate investors will spend endless hours finding a "fundamentally" correct community to invest into.

They'll also search high and low, for days, even weeks, to find a deal. And a deal is usually a property that is

---

slightly run down and beat up. It could use some renovations.

Their belief is that they are "forcing" appreciation on the property by fixing it up. So, the property will be worth tens of thousands more than they bought it for because of the "sweat equity" they put into the property.

By "sweat equity" we mean the work you put in yourself, or with contractors, to improve the condition of the property.

And overall, this is a very good strategy. But here's what's missed.

What is the strategy to get a tenant into the property after the renovations have finished?

Where will the marketing be placed?

How many calls will be expected?

How many people will come out to view the property?

How many offers or applications can you expect for the property?

An investor came into our offices recently because he had bought a run-down property and fixed it up. But he hadn't put much thought into what to do next.

He didn't have a list of available media to advertise in. He didn't have the costs of the advertising worked into his calculations. He didn't know how many people to expect at the property. He didn't even have a good idea of what the property would rent for because he was going to rent the main floor of the house and the basement to separate tenants. So, he really had no clue how long the property would sit vacant.

A vacant property doesn't make money.

In the above example, the investor had the property piece of the formula figured out but didn't have the steps in place to generate revenue.

He was making burgers on his BBQ and not selling burgers using a system like McDonald's.

Your "marketing system" is just as important to your real estate business as the property, if not more so.

You want a repeatable process.

A profitable business is full of systems that when repeated produce an expected result.

1. <u>Leads</u> for Your Properties

Let's focus on generating leads for your properties. The strategies that we'll be discussing have been used for all different types of properties. They've been used for:

A) Single Family Rental Properties
B) Student Rental Properties
C) Lease / Option Properties
D) Multi-Unit Properties

Also, these strategies have been used to "sell" properties as well as "rent" properties.

Any business needs fresh batches of new potential customers. We'll call these "leads." This is your first step in your marketing system.

When setting up this process, you never want one source of leads because if that source stops producing leads your business stops.

You want as many sources of leads as possible. So, part of your role as Chief Marketing Officer for your business is to be constantly on the lookout for ways to generate leads.

There are two primary categories:

1) Online Resources
2) Offline Resources

Online Resources

A) **Kijiji.ca** – Extremely Popular FREE Online Resource

 housing

- apartments for rent
- commercial
- house rental
- housing for sale
- real estate services
- room rental, roommates
- short term rentals
- storage, parking
- other

This is a free classified ad website that has been around for years and is the most popular classified ad website in Canada. We have used Kijiji regularly with great success. You can place free classified ads for your property whether you're buying or selling.

Select the appropriate category from a long list:

Tips: Be aware that when you place your ad on Kijiji.ca, it will be at the top of the pile and get a lot of views and a lot of traffic. However, as other users post their ads on Kijiji.ca your ad will drop and eventually end up on page 2, then page 3, and so on. You can pay a few dollars to have your ad placed back on page one.

Many users avoid the fee by "deleting" their ad and "reposting" it as new. Kijiji.ca has caught on to this practice and will delay the posting of your ad by as much as 24 hours. Overall, it's better to pay a few dollars and have your ad visible at all times. You can also pay slightly more to "peg" your ad to the top of the category for a week.

You can also place ads in many cities across Canada; they're constantly adding more. Make sure you've selected the proper city for your ad. We've noticed that placing it in neighbouring cities will also generate leads.

B)   **GottaRent.com** – Pay per use rental advertising.

Gottarent.com has proven very effective. For approximately $30 a month, we've found it to be the second most effective online resource for lead generation. You can cancel your ad mid-month and get a pro-rated refund. It's mostly used for multi-unit rentals and "regular" single-family home rental properties. If you're leasing out a home using a "lease option" (which we'll dive into detail in Part 4), you'll have to list your property as a regular "rental." There are not "lease/option" or "rent-to-own" options available. However, we've successfully used this website for lease/option properties by putting the details of the lease option in our voicemail message instead of on the website.

C)   **Craigslist.ca** – The Grand Daddy of FREE online classified ads.

This site has been right up there with Kijiji.ca as one of the most used classified sites. It's another great free place to put your ads, and you should be using it when advertising rentals and properties for sale.

D) **Local online newspaper sites** – Almost every single newspaper in Canada will now put your ad online for a very small fee if you place a regular "newspaper" classified advertisement with them. We have rented out many properties from these online sources.

A quick Google search for "classified ads" and your city or town name will turn up other local online resources for you.

Bottom Line: The more exposure your property has, the more leads you will generate. With new online resources popping up almost daily your resources are endless. Become a master of them.

One last point: Some resources are suited very well for specific "types" of properties.

For example, for student rental properties, "off-campus housing" resources associated with the university are your best places to invest.

And for multi-unit properties the most widely used resource is www.ViewIt.ca

Offline Resources

A) **Major Newspapers** – We've found the major newspapers do not generate leads as well as the local papers. So, although they are the obvious places to place your ads you should test and compare for yourself.

Place your ads in the classified section of a major paper and then put an ad in the local community paper. We stopped advertising in the big papers after reviewing the numbers. Test this in your own city.

Every community will require testing. Let's use the example city we've been focusing on, Kitchener, Ontario. Kitchener has a daily newspaper, The Record. And that paper is actually the best place to advertise in. We've tested it against others. However, if you have a property in Mississauga, Ontario (a suburb on the West side of Toronto), you would imagine that its proximity to Toronto would mean that the Toronto Star is the best place to advertise. Our tests showed that the Mississauga News, which is a free community paper delivered 3 times a week, will generate more leads at a lower cost. Conclusion: You must test multiple resources and track results.

B) **Community Newspapers** – these papers usually run between 2 and 3 times a week and are most frequently the best place to generate your ads. Often these newspapers are right under your nose, but you've missed them. A quick Google search will turn them up.

C) **Yard Signs & Directional Signs** – These are surprisingly the most overlooked components of an advertising campaign for properties. You must let people in the community know that you have a property available for rent or for sale. Shocking we know. And don't try and save $100 by using a cheap wire frame for your main yard sign. It'll bend and blow over. Too many investors try to save $100 while trying to make $10,000. Advertising is an investment and should be treated as such. The leads you generate for your real estate investing "business" are worth thousands of dollars to you. One lead may turn into a tenant that rents from you for years.

We'll never forget the story of two brothers who were trying to rent out a home for weeks. They placed some ads but neglected to put a sign on the lawn. After six weeks they decided, at our urging, to put a sign on the lawn. Magically, they rented out the house shortly afterwards, and the tenants commented that they were driving through the area only a few weeks earlier looking for a home to rent!

There are a few things we want to mention here as important components of your online and offline advertising:

- **Voicemail Systems** - We direct all our calls to voicemail systems and then return calls on our schedule. This allows us to live a normal life, without our phones or cell phones ringing at all hours.

  Resource: We highly recommend eVoice.com. For a low cost, you can have a toll-free 1-800 number. You don't need a second phone line to use this service. Voicemail messages are simply emailed to you as an audio attachment in your email. You can then play the messages on your computer at your leisure. This allows for excellent tracking as well.

- **24hr Message** - By tracking responses, we've found that if we include the words "24hr Message" or "Recorded Message" in our ads, it increases our response. This applies to both offline and online ads. So, we record a message about the property on our eVoice.com phone number and then advertise the fact that there's a 24hr message available on every single classified ad or yard sign. We continue to use this strategy in all our ads. This was a huge and very profitable discovery.

2. <u>Appointments</u> For Your Properties.

Once you begin generating leads, the goal is to turn those leads into appointments for your property.

Notice that we didn't say the goal was to "show" your property or to hold an "open house" for your property.

The goal is to get "appointments."

Most investors treat this step very casually and usually guide leads to an "open house." When you do that, here's what you're saying to the person you're speaking with:

"I'm going to be at the house from 2pm-4pm on Saturday whether you show up or not. So, if you remember, and you happen to be in the area, feel free to swing by."

That is not the way to do things. When you go to the dentist, you make an "appointment," and you tend to honour an appointment more than an "open house." There's a feeling of obligation when you commit to an appointment with someone. And that's the feeling you want your leads to have when they meet with you – commitment.

Here's how we suggest you make appointments:

"Hi, I'm calling you back regarding the rental property over on Main Street. We can make an appointment with you to see the property on Thursday at 7:00 pm."

And we then we guide multiple people to the exact same appointment time.

Why?

We want to tilt the playing field in our favour by creating a competitive environment. By having multiple people show up at the same time, we create a sense of urgency for the property.

And it doesn't matter if we're trying to rent the property or sell it. The same psychological triggers are being used.

Think about it...

If a possible tenant is checking out your property, and they are "on the fence" about renting it, wouldn't seeing three other people looking around give them added incentive to make a decision sooner rather than later?

Have you ever been in an electronics store on Boxing Day having a "Blow-Out Sale"? When you're in a store that's crowded with people grabbing things, you are more likely to begin grabbing things as well.

This type of human behaviour has been scientifically measured. If you're interested in learning more about the psychology of persuasion we highly recommend a fantastic book by Robert Cialdini's, *Influence: The Psychology of Persuasion*. It's considered a classic on the topic.

So, remember:

**Multiple People at a Single Appointment Time
= High Application Rate**

A couple of important notes:

- Many investors aren't willing to force all leads to a specific appointment date and time. They're scared that they'll lose leads because some people may not be able to make the appointment time. We can tell you from direct experience that what you lose in lost leads (which will be minimal) you gain in speed at which people make a decision. When multiple parties are viewing a property at the same time people they act faster than if they were the only ones viewing the property. We've seen this time and time again.

- You gain control of your time. Your real estate business shouldn't control you. You should control your business. And the strategy of setting single appointment slots for multiple people gives you control over your schedule. It's your life, remember? Live it on your terms. We can't tell you how many times we've driven to a property to "show it" only to have the people not "show up." The strategy of driving everyone to one time avoids this problem and increases your rate of applications or offers.

Which brings us to our next point…

3. <u>Applications</u> To Rent Or To Buy Your Properties

The only goal of having leads show up at your properties is to either rent it out or to sell it.

If you're renting your property, you want to get as many rental applications as possible.

If you're selling your property, you want as many offers to purchase as possible.

Pretty simple, right?

Many investors get caught up with things like shovelling snow or cutting the grass or fixing a tiny surface crack in a wall. They lose focus. A nicely shovelled driveway or an immaculate lawn can help you, but without applications or offers for your property, you have nothing.

We were working with an investor who was so concerned that the driveway wouldn't be shovelled for leads when they showed up at the property, he cancelled his appointments until he had time to clear the snow. Just a few blocks away, another investor shovelled a tiny path from the street to the front door and rented out his property in days instead of weeks.

Don't hold back appointments until the grass is cut or the snow is shovelled perfectly. Get leads out to the property. **That's where the money is made.**

And when you have leads at the property, all of your focus should be on getting applications.

Here's how to track your effectiveness.

We use a very simple formula to track how well we're doing.

12 Leads = 6 Appointments = 3 Applications

For every 12 leads that we generate from our marketing, we should be able to get 6 people out to the property. And from those 6 people, we should be able to get 3 applications. It's approximately a 50% reduction at each step in the system.

Do you see how our system is starting to take shape?

We've tested this on multiple types of properties, and the formula works exactly the same.

Now, we have a very simple way to measure our work. If we generate a total of 24 leads and after two weeks we only have 2 applications, we know we're not working the marketing system properly.

24 leads should result in 12 appointments at the property and 6 applications. If we end up with 5 applications that's OK, but if we end up with only 2 applications, we begin to examine things like: what we're saying to leads on the phone and in the property and how long we're taking to call leads back and set appointments.

Two common mistakes:

- Not following up with leads fast enough. If you wait more than 48 hours to call your leads back, you'll have a harder time getting through to them.

- Not suggesting that people fill out an application or make an offer. When we were starting out, we often explained how much rent would be but then wouldn't offer a rental application while at the appointment. As soon as we asked that people fill out an application right on the spot, our conversion of leads to tenants increased nicely.

4. Profit From Your Properties

Are you beginning to see that there are two sides to real estate investing? There is the property itself, and there is the marketing of the property.

There's actually a third critical component – management of your property. We'll cover management in future lessons, but for now, the most important concept to understand is that you need a "marketing system" that you can measure and track. It's critically important to your real estate investing business.

Without one, you are wandering around in the dark.

Let's summarize what we've covered and bring it all together:

Leads To **Appointments** To **Applications** Equals **Profit**

And here's how this translates into real-world numbers:

12 Leads
should result in
6 Appointments
should result in
3 Applications
should result in
1 Profit.

You won't always get 1 tenant from 3 applications, but you should have at least one solid candidate to consider. If you're not getting one solid candidate from every 3 applications, then you'll want to examine the source of your leads. You're likely fishing in the wrong pond. Changing your lead generation sources will help correct that.

As you become more experienced in a specific community, you'll be able to tweak these numbers to your local market.

And when you understand your own numbers, you can track your marketing system closely. For example, let's assume that for your properties you actually need to generate 36 leads and get 9 applications to attract the proper tenant.

36 Leads
should result in
18 Appointments

should result in
9 Applications
should result in
1 Profit.

You can then calculate how much money it costs you to generate 36 leads.

Knowing this number is magical because you will know your "cost per sale." Having this knowledge instantly separates you from other investors. 95% of investors do not track this. You may want to add things like your time and travel and other relevant costs to this number.

Let's say it costs you $500 to generate 36 leads. You now know it costs you $500 to generate a new tenant and you can set aside that money in advance for each unit or each property. This way, anytime you have a vacancy, you will know exactly how many leads you need to generate and how much it should cost. If you aren't generating enough leads early on, you can adjust by adding more lead generation sources to your advertising.

Instead of being reactive and without funds (as most investors are) – you are now being proactive and fully funded.

This relieves stress and increases profit.

A good marketing system is priceless. With a steady flow of applications and tenants for your properties, you'll continue to build and snowball your wealth.

And a good marketing system is what turns your real estate investing from a hobby into a business. Master this, and you're on your way.

Chapter 4 Assignments

For Beginners: Start researching the advertising resources in your community. Check out the local newspapers and how often they run. Does the area you are looking to invest in have a daily paper or does it run twice a week? Having this knowledge in advance will allow you to plan for your marketing.

For Experienced Investors: Do you have a vacancy right now? Start using the resources discussed to create your own custom marketing system. Begin tracking where your leads come from and for how much. For example, if Kijiji.ca is generating more leads for a lower cost but the leads who actually rent the property come from Viewit.ca, you'll want to know that.

Chapter 5

Quick Start #4: Professionals

There's no doubt that investing in real estate requires a successful team. There are too many moving parts to be an expert in everything yourself. In fact, there are some things that you just won't be able to do.

There are a lot of tasks a good real estate lawyer performs that can't be done by us, "no law degree" types.

As a real estate investor, we have special challenges to overcome when trying to build our team. They are easy to conquer if you know the tricks, but too many investors have tunnel vision and miss out.

Here is the number one secret tip:

> Building your team of professionals is about
> <u>long-term relationships</u>.

Sounds simple, right?

The problem is, most investors don't think this way. Ask most real estate agents why they don't like working with investors, and you will likely hear similar stories from all of them. Here is one we know of first hand, as our friend was the investor:

Jeff (not his real name) spent thousands of dollars on a weekend real estate boot camp. After the course, he took some time off work because he didn't want his job get in the way of him implementing the strategies to "make millions" he had just learned. So, Jeff called a local real estate agent that he had worked with before because he wanted help looking for the perfect investment property. Over the next week, they spent about 20 hours together looking at properties. They drove to different cities, scouted up and coming areas, and even visited a local planning department together.

Unfortunately, at the end of the week, Jeff still hadn't found exactly what he was looking for. He had found a couple of candidates, but the prices weren't where he needed them to be.

The next week, Jeff was back at work and the images of the 'quick cash' the course spoke about were still flashing in his head. He had a copy of the MLS listings for the homes he visited the week before with his real estate agent, and he got out the one that was closest to what he was looking for.

Do you see what is coming?

He called the agent who had the property listed and asked him a couple of questions about the home. Well, one thing led to another, and before the end of the day, Jeff put an offer in on this house with this new agent.

His offer was accepted, and he was now the new owner of his first investment property.

First, we should congratulate Jeff on taking action. It can be hard to take that first step and purchase an investment property.

But what Jeff realized afterwards was that he sacrificed an extremely good relationship for a very short-sighted reason.

We know it's a long story, but it is an important one, so let us explain by finishing the story.

Jeff thought that by dealing directly with the agent that had listed the property, he would get a lower price. (This can be true sometimes, but from our experience, it is rare.)

In Jeff's story, it was not the case, and the seller paid the same amount of commission, as they would have if he had used his agent who had already spent 20 hours working with him.

Ultimately, Jeff's agent who he had a relationship with learned that Jeff had purchased a home he had spent the time analyzing with him, and understandably he was disappointed that all the time and energy he spent with Jeff would not produce any income.

Jeff went on to renovate this home with the hopes to rent it out afterwards. After the renovations, he needed help and guidance because he was having trouble with some local bylaws and attracting tenants.

He reached out to his real estate agent that had dedicated time to him in the past only to learn that he was busy with other clients who he felt appreciated the service he provided. Politely, he suggested that Jeff contact the agent he purchased the home from since he made income from Jeff's purchase, he should be willing to help him out.

Jeff tried, but that agent was not interested in consulting and admittedly didn't have the expertise Jeff was looking for.

Now he was on his own.

Well, not really because he had friends with investment experience, any ideas who?

Whew... That was a long story. It should help you see the value of building and respecting that knowledgeable team you are looking for.

Jeff took for granted the fact that he was working with a specialist in the types of properties he was looking for.

He also didn't value the time that was put in trying to educate him. Remember, his agent took him to the planning department to teach him about future developments in the area.

How is that for service?

Side note: In most real estate transactions, there are two real estate agents involved. The first is the 'Listing Agent'. This is the agent who has listed the house for sale and represents the seller. Usually, this is the person whose sign will be in the front yard.

The other is the 'Co-operating' or 'Buyer's Agent'. This is the agent who represents the buyer who is purchasing the home.

Typically, they split a set commission rate that is paid for by the seller.

Even if Jeff could have saved $1,000 on the price of the home by going directly to the listing agent so the seller would not have to pay the buyer's agent any commission, it may not have been a wise move.

A long-term relationship with someone that is going to spend the time to educate you, analyze investments, and follow up with you afterwards is much more valuable than minimal cost savings.

It is the long-term relationship that you build with your team of professionals that will increase your investment returns over time.

An important thing to realize is that knowledgeable people who provide good service are not easy to find.

Just in case you think that story sounds a bit self-serving because we have our real estate licenses, here is another quick one to give you a better understanding of what we mean.

This one is a bit different because it is the reverse situation. This is something that happened to us personally.

One of the important pieces to any investment team is a good home inspector, which was harder to find than we had imagined.

Over time, we began to use a particular home inspector regularly. His service was good, and we were happy with the results. However, sometimes he noticed a major flaw with the property very soon after arriving.

He would never mention this to us; he would just continue to do his job, complete the inspection, and then bring it up at the end. Our thoughts, right or wrong, were that if this is a deal breaker and it is noticeable after being at the property for 10 minutes, it might be a good idea to let us know.

It seemed like he didn't value the continuing business we brought and was just out to make his inspection fee every time without actually trying to help us.

We have stopped using him and haven't even gotten a phone call or letter to ask why since then. It's an interesting way to do business, isn't it?

We tested a couple of other inspectors and finally found one that we now use repeatedly. He is much more interested in building a long-term win/win relationship with us.

There have been times where he notices a large issue with a home and asks us if he should continue with the inspection. He has also followed up at properties he never did the inspection for. He seems committed to helping our success, and because of this, we are committed to him.

So, our big lesson about building your investment team around long-term relationships is really a two-way street.

So, how do we build these relationships so that everyone is on the same page?

This is the key question that most investors don't ask themselves, especially in the beginning.

There are two points you need to focus on when starting to work with potential team members.

First, you need to remember "What's in it for them?"

If a mortgage broker is arranging a great mortgage for you, he isn't doing it just from the kindness of his heart. He is looking forward to a commission cheque afterwards so that he can feed his family. That isn't a bad thing; it is the way the world works.

When you close on a deal, your lawyer is going to look out for you and avoid potential pitfalls because he wants to protect himself from potential liability if he makes a large error, and he is looking to be paid.

Too many people complain that some professionals are just in it for the money. This isn't necessarily a bad thing.

Ask yourself why you are investing in real estate? Somewhere in the answer, there is probably a financial goal.

Now it may not just be money that your professionals are interested in, but your job is to understand what it is and respect that.

> "You can have everything in life you want if you just give enough other people what they want" – Zig Ziglar

The goal when building long-term relationships with different professionals is to have it benefit them as well. Any arrangement that is one-sided will fall apart sooner or later, probably sooner.

So, you may want to explain to your handyman that you are in this for the long haul and looking to find someone dependable that does good work. This can serve two purposes. It may motivate him to give great service because he sees future business, and it can also help with pricing because he wants to keep you happy. He might think that since you are using him again, it would be better to not make the price too high because he can make more off of you in the long run.

The key is to live up to your word.

If you promise to use this handyman again, and he gives you good service, do it! You have to keep your end of the bargain as well. Remember, this is a two-way street, right?

This ties in perfectly with the second point you have to remember, and that is, **"Be upfront with your intentions."**

Let's use Jeff's story from earlier as an example.

The experience Jeff went through would be totally different if he would have been upfront with his intentions.

Perhaps he could have toned down the idea that he was going to buy 8 homes in the next year and he wanted to buy multiple ones right away.

If he explained to his real estate agent that he wanted to start checking out homes to get a better understanding of the availability at certain price points, there would have been a better level of understanding.

There is nothing wrong with getting advice from someone and not using their services, but if that is the case, you want to be upfront about your intentions.

For instance, if we were investing in a new area and looking for a handyman, we could let them know that we plan to use 2 or 3 to get an idea of their service levels and then we would like to be able to call one on a regular basis.

We promise you that many more people will respect that approach instead of promising the world and not delivering.

Just the other day we had a conversation with an asbestos specialist over the phone. We were up front with him and told him that we were just exploring some potential ideas. This guy gave us so much information without charging us to come out for a consultation that we had all the answers we needed.

At the end of our chat, we gave him our names and promised any future business we had pertaining to this issue. We're certain that this guy does not remember us at all. But we'll live up to our word and call him before anyone else for this kind of work, even if another contractor falls in our laps.

When we call, we will mention that we had spoken in the past and the reason we were calling back was because of all the great information he gave us, and the fact that we honour our word. We will say this politely, but sometimes it doesn't hurt to remind people you are living up to the things you promised.

Hey, if we don't do it, who will?

Let's do a quick recap.

Here are the two things that most investors overlook when working with professionals.

1) Remember to always think 'what's in it for them?'
2) Be upfront with your intentions

Because so many investors don't do this, you may come across people that have bad experiences before. But you can easily win them over as well by following the two points above.

Now, let's take a look at the types of people that will help you elevate your success. These are the team members you want to be on the lookout for. Some you will need right away, and some can wait.

This isn't a quick process, but it's over the long haul, remember? You aren't a 'flash in the pan' investor -- you will have all the pieces in place.

Home Inspector
Home Inspectors are very easy to find, but like any part of your team, a quality one is hard to find.

Personally, we think this is because the barrier to entry is so low. A few courses and a bit of experience and you can become a home inspector (We might get hate mail for that).

We tried using a home inspector from the Yellow Pages once, and it didn't work out very well. We even tried a home inspector that we met in a real estate office that seemed excellent, but he wasn't very good.

The best experiences we've had were inspectors that were referred to us by knowledgeable people.

Ideally, we want the person that is doing the referring to know more about homes and buildings than we do. Then if they think an inspector is good, usually that means we will think he is great!

After using many different contacts over the years, there are a couple of big points that come to mind.

First, we feel it is important to have an inspector that does a lot of work in the area you are buying. We don't mean, "Yes, I will drive out there to do your inspection," type of work experience. We want him to be doing inspections in the area we are buying on a weekly basis.

Different communities will have different norms and standards. We need our inspector to be familiar with those. Perhaps the area has high water tables, which means the ground around the house will typically be moister than average. This could lead to moisture problems in the basement. So, a small settling crack in the foundation may not be an issue in other areas, but here it could be.

Can you see why that is important?

Exactly, it can save us cash and headaches down the road.

Another trait we've found to be beneficial in home-inspectors is using one that is also an engineer. Most will not be, but we think the benefits are obvious.

You are now using someone with an extra set of specialized knowledge. He can shed more light on potential structural issues and may be able to give you a further understanding of how minor things need to be addressed before they lead to major things down the road.

Caution: Through personal experience, we have noticed that many engineers have a knack for painting the worst possible picture. It is always a good idea to ask them what the realistic scenario is.

One of the most knowledgeable and detail oriented inspectors I've ever met had a tendency to do this.

If we weren't able to read between the lines and come to our own conclusions, he might have talked us out of buying many homes that have made us good money.

For the record, we like engineers. We recommend using them because we think they bring a lot to the table. We're just sharing our personal experiences so you can avoid some of the potential pitfalls.

We hope that saved our friendships with engineers!

Realtor

Like home inspectors, you need to be careful which realtor you build a relationship with.

This might sound strange since we have our real estate broker's license, but we think the same problem that exists with home inspectors impacts real estate agents as well. The barrier to entry is too low. Most provinces, at the time of writing this, simply require you to pass a few exams and you are licensed to sell real estate.

Anyone that has been successful in real estate will tell you that the learning curve takes years and really doesn't ever stop.

As an investor, a good investment focused realtor can be your most powerful ally. The key is finding a realtor that really focuses on the type of investment you are looking for.

When you first speak with a real estate agent, you will probably be asked to sign some sort of agreement binding you to them. This means you are promising that they will be entitled to a commission on any property you buy. We don't really have any issues with those types of agreements, often called a 'Buyer Representation Agreement,' but we would be sure we were signing with the right person.

Before we had our licenses, we weren't interested in signing any sort of agreement binding us to any one individual until they proved their abilities and track record to us. We would always make verbal agreements promising them a commission on any properties they introduced us to, and we stood by our word.

This allowed us to leverage multiple professionals at the same time instead of being locked into one.

There have been a few investors that have come into our brokerage wanting to work with our team but have been unable to because they have signed commitments to other realtors.

That could be viewed as a good or bad thing, but in these cases, they viewed it as a negative. They wanted the flexibility to work with us because they felt that their needs would be better served.

We're not saying this to toot our own horn, but it is important to see that you can get yourself in a bit of a jam if you don't do your due diligence.

To recap, ensure that you are working with realtors that are specialists in your area, and investment type. These are very powerful keys to success.

Bonus: if you want to get creative you can try to have the realtor commit to a bit of assistance with renting or selling the property once it is yours. The time to do this would be just before you buy it as you are in a good negotiating position.

Lender
We'll use the broad term of lender because money for a good investment can come from many different places.

There are three main ones:

Bank – This one is self-explanatory, we hope. Most often people buy real estate by getting a mortgage on the property. This allows them a greater Return on Investment.

There can be some benefits to using a bank to finance your investments, but for beginner investors, those can be very minor. More often than not, the average bank branch will not offer you some of the mortgage options available with mortgage brokers.

We've been in situations where we were teaching the bank's 'mortgage specialist' about their own programs.

We only say this to help you realize that some of these people could be part-time employees that have never had a mortgage of their own. These are not the type of people you want mortgage advice from.

Once you have a good performing portfolio, banks will generally be more interested in making arrangements to get additional business from you.

Mortgage Broker – A mortgage broker can be a great source of financing. They will be able to take your application and put it out to a bunch of different lending institutions.

Some will be banks with branches on the street, and some will be lenders that just have a single office. Often these types of lenders offer more competitive programs than the typical banks.

The benefit to a mortgage broker is that they can shop your mortgage around for the best program that suits your needs.

And here is the great part, it doesn't cost you anything. The bank will pay the fees to the broker. Not bad!

(Like any professional, it is super important that the broker you are working with understands investment mortgages.)

One trick we use is to ask them if they have access to some 'portfolio financing' options. Usually, if they understand that term and can give you some different game plans, they are worth a shot.

<u>Hard Money Lender</u> – This term is thrown around a lot in investment circles. A hard money lender is really just a private individual that is lending you funds, or a group of individuals that have pooled money together to lend to people.

Typically, the interest rates on this type of borrowing will be substantially higher than typical mortgage rates, but the standards for qualifications may be lower as well.

A general rule is that the higher risk of the loan, the higher the interest rate charged will be.

For example, if you are trying to borrow 100% of the price of the home, that is considered a high-risk transaction because there is no equity in the home to protect against market fluctuations.

If you are planning on using these types of lenders, make sure you have a professional review all the documents because there can be some pitfalls you want to be aware of.

As a rule of thumb, we would stay away from hard money lenders unless we had absolutely no other alternative.

A good mortgage broker will also be able to set you up with private loans of this type.

Lawyer

We've heard a lot of jokes about lawyers and the fees they charge, but we can tell you from experience that a good lawyer can really give you a sense of confidence.

Here's a story for you to drive this point home...

After $30,000 of renovations on one of our properties, the couple who bought it tried to come back and sue me (Nick) because there were some things that were original to the home, although my realtor advertised it as 'fully renovated.'

$30,000 goes a long way in a two-bedroom bungalow. It was quite obvious the home was renovated, but there was still some damage to the roof from the owners previous to myself, so I received an unpleasant letter asking me to fix it.

It was very nice having a competent lawyer in my corner that didn't blink an eye in defending me and putting the issue to rest.

Until then, I didn't truly value this relationship.

Many people have an existing relationship with a lawyer who their family has used for years, or maybe a friend of a friend, and they decide to use them for their real estate. Generally, this is a very bad move.

We have seen such arrangements cost investors thousands of dollars – something you want to avoid that!

You should search for a specialist in real estate.

Practicing law is no different than any other profession. If you are not doing something on a regular basis, you start to lose sight of powerful tactics that can be used.

If you know a lawyer that deals with corporate legal issues will they really serve your best interests in the real estate field? They may, but if they don't, it can be a costly lesson to learn.

Find a specialist to ensure that your T's are crossed, and I's dotted.

Accountant
Yes, there are taxes to be paid on money you make! But there are many ways to minimize the amount of tax you owe to the government.

If we mention that you should really find an accountant that specializes in real estate, would you be surprised?

We didn't think so.

Every investor's circumstances will be different, so it is important to have a professional set up the best scenario for you.

Some people will shop around for the cheapest price, but we're more interested in the best service. What good is saving $150 on accountant fees if you have to pay $500 more in taxes?

If you are thinking about owning real estate in corporations, then you will want to come up with a game plan with your accountant.

This is another topic that we will be covering. There is so much in store, we hope you are ready!

Property Manager/Handyman
Depending on how much time and energy you have to put into your investments you may be looking for one or both of these people.

A dependable, local handyman is an invaluable part of the team. We usually check local community papers to try out a couple even for really small jobs, just so we know who to call in the future.

It is nice to be able to offload small tasks to someone right away. Recently, we received a call from a tenant about a broken window. We simply put a call into our handyman, who had it fixed the next day.

The work cost $50, and the tenant paid for it. But, even if we paid for the work, the money would be well worth our time of trying to go out and fix the problem.

If you prefer to fix things like this yourself to save the cash, this may not be an important part of your team. But you may want to find one just in case you want someone on standby for the tasks that you're not interested in.

There is no urgency in finding a handyman, but each time you are in the area, pick up a newspaper or look for signs. As soon as you start searching, you will see ads for handyman services that you never noticed before.

A property manager is a similar role to fill. The type and importance of a property manager is very dependent on the real estate portfolio you are looking to build.

Many beginner investors will manage their own properties at first, so they can have a good understanding of the process. This can be important when setting expectations with a property manager you are thinking about hiring.

If you have low maintenance homes and are willing to take the odd phone call, then this solution might just eat into your monthly cash flow. But if you are looking for a complete, hands-off approach, a management company becomes essential.

At no time will referrals or references be more important than with property management companies. Taking the time to speak with past clients about their experiences will be worth it. A bad property manager can cost you a lot of money very quickly.

And any company that has faith in the service they provide will gladly have some references on hand.

The Nosy Neighbour
This generally isn't one person, whenever we have a chance we always try to get to know a neighbour close to each one of our properties.

Here is our method of finding one:

When you first take ownership of the property, pay close attention the first couple of times you visit.

You will usually see the same person on their lawn or porch monitoring your every move. Most often it is someone trying to protect the integrity of their neighbourhood, which is exactly what you are looking for.

This person will often be willing to lend a helping hand by shovelling snow and cutting grass. Plus, they will usually watch out for your home, and let you know anything that may interest you about it.

We like nosy neighbours!

Plus, the best part is that someone is keeping an eye out for your home is free!

Phew, this chapter was an extra long one, so let's take a deep breath and have a quick recap. In point form to keep it short.

- We know that real wealth in real estate comes from long-term outlook, so we want to build long-term relationships to complement our vision.

- When working with professionals, remember to keep in mind what they will get from working with you. Make it a win/win relationship.

- Keep your word. You never know when you will need that person's services again.

- Look for specialists! Any old pro won't do for us. We want investment real estate focused people. The more investment experience they have, the better.

- Look for recommendations when building your team. The chances of a great investment real estate lawyer knowing a similarly skilled accountant are very good.

Remember, no championship team is built in one shot. There are a lot of trades and free agent signings along the way to find the perfect combination.

Your team will be formed the same way. It will take some time.

But just like any wise businessperson, you should **begin with the end in mind.**

Chapter 5 Assignments

For Beginners: Start looking for investment professionals in your area. The real estate investment world is smaller than you think. After a bit of research, the same names will begin appearing, often those are the winners. Reach out to them, and explain who you are and your long-term vision and goals. Often their responses to your initial contact will give you a better idea of who they are.

Experienced Investors: Take a step back and re-evaluate your team. Make sure every person on it is still the best person for your specific goals.

Chapter 6

The "Magic Snowball" That
Keeps Your Portfolio Growing

According to Dictionary.com, the verb "snowball" means "to cause to grow or become larger, greater, more intense, etc., at an accelerating rate: to snowball a small business into a great enterprise."

In terms of your real estate investing empire, it's the ability to roll one investment into a second and then into a third, fourth, fifth, and so on.

There are MANY different ways to do this that we'll be discussing through the book, but today we want to give you one of the easiest ways to "snowball" your investments.

The best strategy of all…

Turn One House into Two, and

Two into Four, and on and on and on…

This strategy is truly magical because it begins to take on a life of its own.

We receive a LOT of feedback, questions, comments, and real estate investing "flavours of the day." And the most successful investors who contact us have been following the strategy of "turning one house into two, and two houses into four, and so on...."

Let's study this process...

See the house in the picture above. This is a satellite shot of a house that we still own just outside Toronto, Ontario.

We purchased this house for $250,000. It was a private sale, and we really didn't know how to handle private sales at the time.

We rented out the house for $1,500, and we rented out the basement apartment for $850 for a total of $2,350 a month.

We had fluctuating carrying costs because of changing interest rates, but on average it has been cash flowing at approximately $845 per month – every month!

Let's take a look at the numbers on this property…

$2,350.00
-1,245.00 (loan payment – two loans for a total of $225,000)
- 200.00 (property taxes)
- 60.00 (insurance)
= $845.00 in monthly cash flow

This house generates $10,140 in income per year.

After owning the house for just over two years, the real estate market happened to be in one of its "upswings."

This allowed us to refinance the house and extract $30,000 in equity from the house.

We used the $30,000 + $10,140/year in income to:

1. "Invest" back into the property by updating one of the washrooms and both kitchens. We strongly believe in keeping our properties in good condition. In the long run, it creates more value for you and attracts better tenants.

2. "Save" $35,000 to purchase another property.

With the $35,000 and with the help of our family, who found this beauty, we tracked down and purchased a beautiful semi-detached property on the north side of Toronto.

It was a semi-detached home in a very desirable area that was bought brand new from a new home builder.

Note: One of the most important things we did to this property was to build a separate entrance to the basement in the backyard so that we could rent it out as a separate apartment.

This house happens to be very close to a major university so our thought process was to rent out the top of the house to students and the self-contained basement apartment to a Professor or Teaching Assistant.

Having the separate entrance really made it attractive to anyone renting out the basement. And because the area is in demand we are able to get a gross rent of $2,800 for the house and $1,200 for the basement – for a total of $4,000 per month in rent. We purchased the property for $350,000.

Let's take a look at the numbers on this next property...

$4,000.00
-1,956.00 (loan payment)
- 250.00 (property taxes)
- 180.00 (insurance is high because the house is considered a "student rental")
- 700.00 (we pay for internet access, phone, utilities, etc. on this property)
= $914.00 in monthly cash flow

After owning this property for two years, we were able to refinance it and extract approximately $108,000.

We hit an appreciation in prices relatively early in owning this property. Part of the reason we were able to extract as much cash as we did was because we purchased it very early on from the builder at "pre-construction prices." Real estate was appreciating during the 18 months it took to take possession of this property and then continued to appreciate for the first two years of ownership.

Important: You never know when real estate is going to go through an "upswing" – we always buy real estate for "income" and not for "appreciation." We patiently wait for the appreciation but don't expect it or become frustrated if it doesn't occur in the first couple of years.

Back to our story...

We were then able to take this cash and purchase two homes for approximately $250,000 each about an hour west of Toronto.

It is a small single-family home that is leased out using a lease/option strategy. It generates $200/month in positive cash flow and we were able to collect just over $10,000 from the tenant/buyer before they moved in. The tenant/buyer pays for utilities.

The next property we purchased was a four-level side-split that we also rented out using a lease/option strategy. This house generates $300 in positive cash flow per month. The tenant/buyer pays for utilities.

And for this particular property, we actually had found a tenant ready to rent the property before we even purchased the property. So, we were able to collect just over $8,000 from them before we waived the financing and home inspection conditions from our offer.

We also lined up the closing date with the exact date that the tenant would move in. So, the day we picked up the keys, we handed them off to the tenants and drove home. Isn't that a nice way to invest!

Chapter 7

The Most Important Key to Success in Real Estate

It is pretty obvious that there are a lot of ways to invest in real estate. We touched on many of the different tactics and types of properties in the first few chapters.

In the coming chapters, we are going to use real life, up to date, case studies to dive into the different types of investments.

We will drill right down into the profit numbers of each case study to see how it can fit into your "snowball."

The biggest challenge for most investors is figuring out where to start or where they are heading.

This lesson applies to all investors, whether you've yet to invest or you've been investing for ten years.

It really isn't anything earth-shattering. Actually, it is a simple concept, but sometimes we forget the basic KISS principle.

K – Keep
I – It
S - Simple
S – Sally - some people say 'stupid,' but that's not nice!

The key to success in any real estate portfolio is **focus**. Let us explain:

For beginners, it can be easy to get swamped with information from different sources.

You do a bit of research about investing, and your idea slowly changes from the one-bedroom condo you were going to rent out to owning the next big box retail shopping centre.

You watch a bit of late night TV and see someone in the US that "made" $30,000 by renovating a home you wouldn't dare live in and selling it, all within a month. That sounds great and seems straightforward enough, so you want to rush out and find the most distressed property you can find.

We understand because we've been there!

The dollar signs start flashing in your eyes until you speak with a friend of a friend that owns three student rental properties, all generating $1,200 a month is cash flow (a very real number). You think, "That's $3,600 a month. I can quit my job!"

Now you have plans to be the student rental king of the closest university town.

Maybe you have passed that point, and you're a more experienced investor.

You have one condo that you rent out that is $50 a month negative in cash flow (because it was your first one and a learning experience).

You also have a triplex that has worked out OK, but you aren't a big fan of dealing with the tenants regularly. However, the triplex produces cash flow, which has been great, so you have seen the benefits of real estate investing.

You decided to move on to a student rental because you are now hooked on cash flow, but you can't stand to go into the home because it is generally unkempt with dust balls along both sides of the hallways, and some interesting green stuff on the cheese in the fridge.

> You see it doesn't matter what type of investor you are or how many properties you have. Your success will only be increased by having **focus**.

Focus on the types of investments that fit into your lifestyle and focus on your long-term goals.

We all invest in real estate for a reason. For most people, it has to do with some sort of financial freedom.

We personally call this reason "Living Your Rock Star Life," which is living your life on your terms.

As an investor, you need to focus on a long-term plan because that acts as your guide when acquiring your investments.

For example, let's pretend you are looking at creating $3,500 a month in passive income. You want to do this, so you don't feel as dependent on your 9-5 job, or you're looking to create long-term, generational wealth. Good stuff! But with these goals, trying to flip a property does not get you to where you want to be.

Even if you were successful in flipping the property, that would be a short-term solution to a long-term problem.

When speaking with other investors, this topic often comes up because too few people set a bar for themselves to reach. Afterwards, they often tell us that they need to sit down and evaluate their investments to see if it is taking them to their ultimate goal.

Consistent focus is not easy.

Let's face it, we all get excited by the next shiny object that comes along.

It doesn't matter if it's the latest flat screen TV or an investment that seems better than your own. These things can easily get us to veer off the course we set for ourselves.

Some experienced investors have revamped the type of investments they have because they realized that along the way they lost sight of what they were striving for.

Let's use me, Nick, as a guinea pig. Sound good?

When I started investing, my goal was to create passive income. So, what did I do? I went out and bought this....

This is a two bedroom bungalow with

one and a half bathrooms. There was a crack in the foundation so big you could literally see daylight through it.

I have fond memories of this home since it was my very first investment property.

Let's take a quick look at the timeline of this investment.

1. Took possession of the property at the beginning of April.
2. Had workers start repairing the foundation the same day (I thought I was smart).
3. Spent all my spare time, plus a lot of my father's, fixing up the home over the next 8 weeks.
4. Listed the home for sale at the end of May (it was a birthday present to myself).
5. After finally understanding the real estate agent wasn't well versed in the area, I took charge of the sale, and it sold in early July.
6. The buyers took possession of the home at the end of August.

Purchase Price: $158,000
Sale Price: $209,000

Profit: Nowhere near what it looks like from those numbers. After all was said and done, I made myself about $4,000, but I learned A LOT!

I kept the story short because there were countless lessons that I learned….and I mean countless. <u>But here is the biggie</u>.

Even if I made $10,000, this type of investment wasn't getting me to my goal. I wasn't focused on what I was trying to accomplish, which was long-term, passive income.

If I was, I would not have decided to try and flip a property.

So, you can see that I didn't have focus from the beginning. I was just trying to do what I thought was real estate investing.

At the end of the day, after the property was sold, I no longer had any real estate, and I wasn't any closer to my long-term goal. I needed to refocus.

Do you see how easy it can be to jump on an opportunity just because you think it is good, even though it doesn't fit with what you are trying to accomplish?

In this story, I was a new investor, but the same thing happens to countless experienced investors, maybe even more so.

For some reason, we seem to have a tendency to move away from things that we have made work for ourselves. As investors, we are always looking for more, right? We want to top our last investment.

This is a great trait if we can keep the focus on the long-term goal and make the investment congruent with it.

Intentional congruency is a fancy term I learned from Nido Quebin, who I highly respect. Here is the definition of congruence:

"Congruence – agreement, harmony, conformity."

So intentional congruency is when we purposely try to introduce new things in our lives that will enhance what we have already established.

Let's use another example.

Let's pretend you have the same long-term focus as me, and that is <u>passive income</u>.

You have taken the first step and own a six-unit building with tenants in it. You have gone through the learning curve of managing a building, and you have a marketing system in place to attract tenants.

Congratulations, you are doing well!!

You have some extra money to invest, and you would like some more real estate.

Your friend tells you of a great condo in Florida that is being sold under market value and 'has to' go up over time.

Maybe they are right, but if you step back and focus on your long-term intentions, would the Florida investment get you closer?

If it does great, but if realistically it will become a distraction, it may be best to stay away.

If it didn't bring you closer, what would?

You have already mastered the management of a building and have a marketing system in place, right?

So, as the saying goes, "why fix what ain't broke?"

You may be better served by looking for another six-unit building. That way, you can leverage what you have to make both investments more successful.

One of our private coaching clients emailed us about this topic. Here is what he said about this principle of focus.

"5 years ago, I experienced the same dizziness, where to start and what is the next step? I wish this article was available to me at that time. But better late than never..."

Isn't it great when you can learn from other people's experiences and save 5 years?

Just think, if you learn this one trick to investing, you can cut your learning curve by A LOT!

It's amazing how the most basic things can be the most important.

Once you have focused on your objective, we will need to focus on the best investment vehicles to get you there.

Duplexes, student rentals, lease options, wholesaling, etc. all have different levels of responsibilities involved. Keep this in mind when narrowing your focus.

Side Note: Remember, investing in real estate has a couple other parts other than cashing cheques every month (Although when we arrive at the bank on the first of the month with a bunch of rent cheques to cash, it <u>always</u> brightens up our day.).

You want to keep in mind how much of the responsibility you are willing to handle. Most investors will take care of it all when they start out and then slowly transfer over to some sort of repair and management system or company.

This will also determine which property types you want to **focus** on.

Some of the most successful investors only invest in one type of property because they are good at it and the returns meet their needs.

That's it for Part 1. From here we take a deep dive into all the investments listed above.

We are going to cover them one by one starting in Part 2.

We're purposely taking it one step at a time, so you skip out on years of "dizziness."

Chapter 7's Assignment

You're starting to pour the foundation to your empire, big or small. Grab a coffee, tea, or even a glass of wine and think about what you are trying to accomplish with your real estate investments.

What is your ultimate goal of investing in real estate?

What kind of lifestyle do you want with these investments?

How much day-to-day responsibility are you willing to handle?

The answers to these questions can act as a mini business plan for you. If you already have some investments, revisit the profit and the work involved and ask yourself if these fit in with your goals.

Part 2:

Beyond The Basics

Chapter 8

Sometimes Investing Can Be Boring

When most people hear the term "real estate investing," they associate the word "landlord" with it right away.

To many people, "landlord" brings images of lying underneath a kitchen sink to repair a leak, instead of realizing the generational wealth that rental properties can provide.

For our purposes in this chapter, let's use a single-family detached home as our example property.

It is important to realize that a "rental property" could also be a semi-detached home, townhome, condominium, etc. The information we cover here applies to all those types of properties.

Before we go any further, let's take a step back.

In an earlier chapter, we went through the idea of owning a group of assets that pay for themselves and create some monthly cash flow for you. Truthfully, there aren't many of these types of assets available.

Self-Liquidating Asset - *"An asset that generates adequate income to return the total amount of its cost."*

Self-liquidating assets are how people become wealthy. It takes time; this isn't a get rich quick 'Ponzi' scheme. Investing in real estate is a process.

A very proven process! Let's use a quick example.

A rental property is similar to buying a business. If you were to buy a business, we hope your goal would be to have the business produce a positive income.

You would want enough money to pay all your expenses like rent, salaries, and inventory. You would also want money left over to recoup the money used to buy the business or to pay back the loan. Plus, for all this work you need a piece of the pie, right?

A successful business is a perfect example of a self-liquidating asset.

Take a minute and think of all the wealthiest people you know, or have read about in the media. How many of them are business owners?

Chances are about 75% of them would be. That's because owning assets that pay for themselves and produce income is the longest running, most proven, and most consistent way to increase your net worth.

Do you see any similarities between a good business and a good rental property? Obviously, we can see that the same principles apply, right?

The one big difference is that there is less daily management of a long-term rental property. It usually shifts in and out of autopilot, which is why it is so much fun.

A rental property is often someone's first step into real estate investing. Often it is because it is perceived as a less risky investment.

The typical thought process is that there shouldn't be as many surprises. You buy a home, rent it out, and cash cheques. Easy as pie!

There are definitely more steps involved, and because rental properties are a cornerstone to any long-term real estate portfolio, we will be covering these steps in more details in the next few chapters.

First, you need to know that owning a rental property is not very flashy.

There are not many TV shows made about people renting out properties for good monthly income. It can be considered a bit boring, and that is a good thing. In fact, with rentals, the truth is, *"the more boring, the better."*

If there is no action, it means there are no major events at the property except for collecting a monthly cheque that you get to deposit, which is perfect.

Here is a picture of us in front of one of our rental properties.

This is an old photo as we've owned this home for many years now, and there is no fascinating story for us to tell you about this place.

We have had a tenant in there paying us rent every month. Although he was late a few times, there have been no major incidents.

Here's why.

We picked a home that had at least one unique advantage over the other homes in the area at the same price point.

This area, like many older neighbourhoods, had a high number of 3 bedroom bungalows. That is considered the norm. This home has 4 bedrooms all 'above grade', which means none of them are in the basement. This means that it can appeal to a larger number of families.

We purchased this property for the same price as many of the 3 bedroom bungalows in the area.

This was our **unique advantage**. We could advertise a 4-bedroom home for the same price the 3 bedroom homes were renting at and still make money.

We didn't just go out and buy the first home we liked, crossed our fingers that someone else would like it too and hope they paid us rent. We did a bit of market research. Here are the steps we took:

1) We performed some Rock Star TNT (from Chapter 2).

This means that we did our research to find what we considered to be a fundamentally strong area. We used the

Rock Star TNT approach to look at different trends for the area.

We looked at trends in vacancy rates, population, employment, and migration.

Once we were satisfied with what we knew we took the next step.

2) We looked at 'real life' rental rates in the area.

CMHC produces rental reports that cover some vacancy and pricing trends. But these trends didn't apply to us because they were for apartments.

None of the information applied to the type of investment we were after which was a single-family rental (detached, semi-detached, townhome).

So, we needed to do our own research. We used Realtor.ca, which was the system we had access to. We covered this in Chapter 3.

Using this, we could see what the asking prices were for different rental properties in the area. We were also able to see the pictures, which gave us a vague idea of what condition the property was in.

3) We crunched some numbers.

Once we got a general idea of the rental rates, we needed to figure out what purchase price those rents would support.

For example, we needed the rent to cover our monthly mortgage payment, property tax, and home insurance with some extra cash flow left over for us.

(Remember we are after a self-liquidating asset. That principle is what makes these homes act like our very own ATM.)

If rents in the area were $1,500, we couldn't be looking at $400,000 homes.

4) We did some "on the streets" research.

Once we knew our conservative rents and had an idea of the price range of home we were looking at, it was time to get away from the computer and see the real thing.

Although the Internet makes investing a lot easier, there is no substitute for actually seeing properties yourself. Sometimes you won't be able to understand how the pictures can look so good when you arrive to find a home that needs a lot of work.

This picture is of a property we were interested in. The numbers worked out OK, and the initial pictures online didn't look too bad either.

The owner must have "forgotten" to take a picture of this area, and some others that needed quite a bit of work.

Yes, this example is a bit extreme, but we think it gets the point across. We guess a picture really is worth 1,000 words!

There are two types of "on the streets" research you need to do.

First, you want to look at other rental units in the area. It is amazing how many people will skip this step and look for their own property right away.

Scouting out some current rentals at different price points will give you the competitive intelligence you need.

Tips for Scouting Other Rental Properties

- How much is the rent?

- How long is the required rental period?

- How long has it been vacant?

- What kind of condition is the property in?

- What distinguishing features does the property have?

When you go through other rental properties, pay specific attention to what these places offer so you can look for your **unique advantage**.

For example, if all the rental units in the area have carpet throughout the home, then some hardwood in the living room and dining room places your home above the rest.

Another example could be a bathroom in the basement. That will definitely, attract more interest than properties that don't have one.

This is an important step. Scouting your competition will give you the information you need to make sure you are ahead of the pack.

Now that you know what the rentals in the area are like, it is time to move on and scout the homes for sale.

The reason to scout homes for sale is to get an idea of what price points different homes are at. After you look at 10 to 15 homes, you will start getting a good idea of the values in the neighbourhood.

You also want to seek out homes that will give you that **unique advantage**, whatever it will be for you, an extra bedroom or bathroom, some upgraded features such as hardwood, or anything else that will set your property above the standard rental available.

You can see that there was some behind the scenes work to do before we jumped in. But it's not work when you love it!

We believe this information is what helps us rent and manage the property successfully, and it will do the same for you.

You now know what the standard rental properties are like so when you are showing yours, you can be confident in the home and your pricing.

If a potential tenant comes in and tells you that your rent is high compared to homes down the street, you know they are either fibbing, or the homes with low rent have a good chance of being "dumps."

You're prepared to start evaluating single family, residential rental properties. Remember, these lessons apply to different types of homes, not just the detached homes we used in the examples.

If you were renting out condominiums, you would use the same steps to educate yourself on the market. You will have the inside track to success.

Chapter 8's Assignment

Complete the four steps above for the rental area or areas you are considering. Some areas will have a higher monthly cash flow potential than others.

Chapter 9

Number Crunching for Single Rental Units

Like any investment, one of the most important things to us, as the investor, is the potential to make a solid return on our money.

It's not rocket science, right? The ultimate goal is to put some money in and have more money come out. What a great feeling!

Before you go into any real estate investment, you should definitely "crunch the numbers" on the property.

By "crunch the numbers" we mean, calculate the expenses and projected income for the property.

It is very important to be **conservative** when you are evaluating a potential investment.

Today we are still focusing on a single-family rental property, and there are two ways money travels with a rental property.

"In" and "Out."

We are going to focus on our expenses or the money going out first.

There are two parts to this…

Expenses – Part 1: The Monthly Commitment

As the owner of the property, you are responsible for paying certain bills every month.

- Mortgage Payment
- Property Taxes
- Home Insurance
- Utilities (optional depending on the way your lease is structured)

We use a very simple spreadsheet when we are evaluating a property. Here's a quick look at part of it.

Down payment	20%
Interest rate:	3.5%
Purchase Price	$390,000.00
Down Payment	$78,000.00
Mortgage Insurance	$0.00
Mortgage Amount	$312,000.00
Monthly Mortgage Payment	$1,557.72
Taxes & Insurance	$370.00
Utilities	$0.00
Total Payment	$1,927.72

These are the basic monthly costs that you would be responsible for if you owned this property. There are a few points to make:

Interest Rate: This rate changes often. You will need to contact your mortgage broker or banker to check what the current interest rates are when you run your numbers. That way you can get a more accurate 'Total Payment" number.

Mortgage Insurance: In Canada, you must get mortgage insurance for any mortgage in which the bank is not given a 20% down payment. This amount does not come directly out of your pocket, but it actually gets added on to the mortgage.

By getting the mortgage insurance added on to the mortgage, it will change your carrying 'Total Payment' slightly.

We have not included it in this example because it can vary depending on the type of investment mortgage you decide to use. Different banks have different programs available to investors, but good brokers are your best bet as less than 20% down is difficult to find in today's world.

Big Tip: Some investors will borrow money from private lending sources to increase the amount of down payment they have available.

This allows them to minimize or eliminate any mortgage insurance fees.

They would then work in a monthly 'interest only' payment to their private money lender as part of their total 'Monthly Payment' for the investment property

---

Utilities: We typically arrange for the tenants to pay utilities, so this expense was left at $0. If you plan to rent out the property and cover all utility costs, you would include the cost of gas, hydro, and water services here.

Don't forget that you will be responsible for the utility payments whenever the home is vacant as well.

Often your monthly costs are also referred to as your 'carrying costs' for the property.

The goal of any rental property is to have 'positive cash flow' which is more money coming in every month than going out.

That is why establishing your carrying cost is the first step when evaluating any rental property. There is one important thing that was left out.

Maintenance: Any time you own property, there is a chance of a maintenance issue arising. The longer you own the property, the greater the chance that repairs will be needed.

The R word (repairs) is what scares away many investors. But they really aren't bad. Plus, if your rents are structured correctly, you will have ample income to cover any costs that should come up.

Different investors will use varying amounts when they are estimating monthly repairs. The range can be really wide depending on the type of property and its condition.

For example, this is a picture of a condominium townhome that is used as a rental property in B.C.

With this property, the amount set aside for maintenance

would be very low because most of the major expenses would be covered by the monthly condo fees (roof, windows, front door).

But the maintenance would be very different on this detached home in Ontario. In this example, you would need to cover the cost of the maintenance issues that come up.

And if you plan on holding the property for a long time it is normal to have some standard repairs.

But if we take the long-term vision into account, and plan accordingly, the impact will be limited.

For a home in good condition, it is probably a good idea to set aside at least $50 per month for some minor maintenance issues.

Expenses – Part 2: The Initial Investment

Now that we have worked out our monthly costs, it is time to look at the other big expense we are responsible for with a rental property. That is our initial investment.

We want to make sure that this investment is going to provide us with the return we are looking for.

Here's how the expenses break out in our example.

	Down payment	20%
Down Payment		$78,000.00
Closing Costs		$5,000.00
Advertising		$500.00
4 months carrying costs		$7,710.88
Out of Pocket Investment		$91,210.88

Let's go over a couple of the key points to make sure we are on the same page.

Closing Costs – This term typically refers to the amount of money it takes to have the property transferred to your name and a mortgage registered against it.

There are many costs that can fall into this category, but the most common ones are taxes and legal fees. The Land Transfer Tax amount can vary depending on what province and city you live in. Also, the exact amount of legal fees can vary depending on the lawyer you use.

You will receive an exact breakdown of all the fees from your lawyer when you are completing the paperwork.

The $5,000 used above is broken down to about $3,000 in tax and the rest to legal fees, so we should not be far off.

> **BIG TIP:** Here is the clause we have used over 200 times.
>
> "The vendor agrees to pay the purchaser's closing costs for a total of $5,000, and further agrees to permit the said sum to be shown as a credit to the purchaser on closing. The vendor and the purchaser hereby acknowledge and agree that the aforementioned payment does not form any part of the purchase price."
>
> **Disclaimer:** We should let you know that the bank will need to agree to accept this clause, and although we have used it with many banks in Canada and many of the smaller lenders, they could change their policies at any time.

Advertising – It is not often that you buy a rental property, and people just start knocking on your door to start paying you rent.

It is rare that we spend $500 on advertising. Usually, a tenant has moved in before we get to that point. But remember we are trying to work with realistic numbers, so let's play it safe.

4 Months Carrying Costs – This is a big one that most people leave out. Most of the time we know that a tenant will not be moving in the same day we take possession of the property, so we have to expect to make a couple monthly payments without rent coming in.

Sometimes we will buy a property with two months' rent in hand before we take possession, and a tenant lined up to move in as soon as we close on the property. But, that is for a future chapter!

We use four months of carrying costs because often, even if we find a tenant in the first couple of weeks, they will have to give some vacancy notice at their current home. So, they may not be able to move in right away.

Now, it's time to pull these expense numbers together with some income to get an idea of the profit potential that we see.

Although investing in real estate in fun, there is some work involved too, so the return on our investment is always important.

Once again, the total monthly payment would be $1,927.72 with 20% down.

With costs like this, we would likely be investing in a home that could generate about $1,800 to $2,000 in monthly rent as a minimum.

This way if we put 20% down on the property we would have positive cash flow to cover maintenance, plus a good return on the investment we made.

If we were generating $1,950 per month in rent and paying out $1,927,72 that would give us a difference of **$22.28** per month, which would be our **positive monthly cash flow**.

But there are a couple of other sources of income that come with a rental property. Take a look.

Out of Pocket Investment	$91,210.88
1st Year Monthly Cash flow	$267.36

1st Year Mortgage Pay Down	$7,979
1st Year ROI	9.04%

Mortgage Pay Down – Every time you collect rent from a tenant and pay your mortgage with it, you will owe less to the bank. This is because, with every mortgage payment, you are repaying part of the loan that you took, pretty simple.

That means there will be more equity in the rental property as each month passes, so it can be looked at as a source of income.

ROI (Return on Investment) – This is the percentage of the money you are making back on your initial investment. Here is how the calculation looks.

Yearly Profit ÷ Out of Pocket Investment = Return on Investment

In this example, this is how it would look.

Profit [Cash flow **($267.36)** + Mortgage Pay down **($7,979)**] **Divided by** Out of Pocket Investment **($91,210.88)**

Remember, one of the biggest benefits of investing in real estate is that it allows you to take this profit without having to sell the asset.

And because you still have the asset (property), you have more control over how these numbers look.

Small changes to the rental numbers can make a big difference on your overall return on investment.

Here's a quick example.

If we successfully negotiate to have the seller pay our closing costs in this example our 'Out of Pocket Investment' drops to $86,210.88.

Out of Pocket Investment (without closing costs)	$86,210.88
1st Year Monthly Cash flow	$267.36
1st Year Mortgage Pay Down	$7,979
1st Year ROI	9.6%

By having our closing costs paid for by the seller, we have managed to increase our potential return on investment by 0.5%.

Another thing that we should remember is that in the early period of a mortgage more of your monthly payment is being put towards interest. As the years go on and your mortgage is paid down a larger portion of the monthly payment will be applied to the loan amount.

This means that your yearly cash flow numbers will look better and better as each year goes by. And we are already starting at about 10%.

Fun stuff, right?

And don't forget that your investment is secured against the property. This is extra special when you take into account the appreciation that will occur with the price of the home.

Let's do one last calculation of our investment, but this time we will add in a small amount of appreciation.

House prices in each market will move at different rates. Over a long-term period, the prices have continued to rise because of a number of factors including inflation.

In our example, we will use a modest 3% price increase. Depending on your area this could be much higher.

Here is how our return looks with some appreciation added to the $390,000 rental property we have been looking at.

Out of Pocket Investment (without closing costs)	$86,210.88
1st Year Monthly Cash flow	$267.36
1st Year Mortgage Pay Down	$7,979
Appreciation (3%)	$11,700.00
1st Year ROI	23.14%

Even if we look at the possible appreciation as a bonus, it will become a factor during the time you own your property if you are in for the long haul.

Perhaps the best part about this investment example is that **you still own the property**. Your initial investment is secured against the piece of real estate you have invested in.

It is a <u>self-liquidating asset</u> that is paying for itself and spitting off some cash.

Kind of like your own private ATM.

<u>Chapter 9's Assignment</u>

Take the properties you were working with in the last chapter and crunch the numbers. Remember to be conservative with your estimates to ensure the projections are realistic. How do they look? Keep in mind any maintenance issues that may need to be addressed.

(You may need to speak with a mortgage broker to see what the best interest rates or investment options are for you right now. This will give you the information you need to crunch the numbers.)

If you would like, email one of your potential properties to us at **TomAndNick@rockstarinnercircle.com** and we can provide you with some quick feedback.

Chapter 10

5 Things That Might Be Holding You Back

Over the years, we've received thousands of questions about our investing strategies. While we've received some very interesting one-off questions (you'll find an example of one of these below), there are a few questions we're asked over and over again. So, in this chapter, we're going to tackle some of the most frequent questions that come into our office.

Question #1: Are some areas of a city better than others when you are searching for rental properties?

This is a great question because it can impact the demand for your property. There are some things to look for when scouting investments property areas. The goal is to find an area where the demand is the highest.

In an earlier chapter, we covered selecting the types of cities and areas to invest in, but this question applies to a smaller, block by block area.

There are some areas that are better to invest in and it all comes down to what people want.

We guess we should clarify that point. Yes, many people want to live in a 5,000 square foot mansion, but it usually doesn't make the best rental property for our purposes.

Some 'wants' will be standard features people find appealing and some will be specific to tenants.

Here are some of the things we look for in the immediate area of our single-family rentals.

Transportation – This breaks down into a couple categories. The first is public transportation.

The closer your home is to a major public transportation artery the more valuable it becomes for two reasons.

A 'major public transportation artery' would be a subway or train system or a major bus route. If you are in the suburbs there can sometimes be a bus route that only runs for a couple hours in the morning and evening of each day during high traffic periods. This would not benefit you as much as being within a quick walk of a main route that has frequent service throughout the day.

Some Canadian and US studies have shown that historically being within 800 metres of a subway, train, or light rail transit station will cause your home to appreciate at a faster rate than the homes outside of those areas.

The second reason is that it will create more demand for your property allowing you to charge premium rents.

The second transportation category is access to highways. This one is pretty simple.

The convenience of being within a quick drive to a highway is something that is appealing to most people. It can give us quick access to work, malls, family, friends, etc.

If we had to decide between two similar properties and one was 15 minutes away from the highway while the other was 5, the closer one would win out almost every time (except if we negotiated a super price on the one further out!).

Density – we are much more interested in rental properties in urban areas than ones on the outskirts of town. Remember, we look to **buy into demand**.

Since there are more people and jobs in densely populated areas, it is appealing.

We have had opportunities to snap up some properties in rural areas at good prices with a tenant in place and passed up on them.

You must think ahead. If the tenant leaves, how are you going to find another one if the home is on a farm, 30 minutes away from the city, compared to a small townhome in the city centre?

Your property does not have to be in a major metropolitan area but it really helps to be in an area with a good population base.

General Area Appeal – Often there will be good rental demand and cash flow positive properties available in less desirable neighbourhoods. Sometimes these areas are less maintained and have an elevated crime rate.

We think every city has some pockets like this when it grows. We stay away from them because even though the numbers may look good on paper there are other factors to consider, the primary one being the demand for the property.

We prefer to have our properties in areas that people look to aspire to live. Areas where the majority of homes are well maintained and there is pride in the community.

As a general rule, if you don't feel comfortable walking down the street at night by your rental property, why would someone else?

Every investor will have his or her own preference in the small details they look for. Things like proximity to parks, schools, and stores often are a factor for people. But our experiences have told us that these are less of a factor for renters than the three areas we covered above. Your experiences might teach you otherwise.

If you follow the guidelines, you'll be in good shape.

Question #2 – Would condominium units in high rises work as investments?

They would be great!

Next question!

It would be nice if all answers were so simple, but there are a couple of things to consider.

Our ultimate goal is always to have positive cash flow properties. This is what will carry us through market fluctuations.

The challenge with condominiums is that often the monthly condo fees make it difficult to generate a positive cash flow from the unit. So, it really comes down to the crunching the numbers on the potential investment to see how it will work out.

Remember, your monthly carrying costs will largely depend on your down payment. So, there will be a greater cash flow with a higher down payment.

Often this is the key to making a condominium create good, positive, cash flow.

There can be some HUGE advantages to using these as investment properties, and they revolve around maintenance.

Yes, you are responsible for condo fees every month, but there is a lot less maintenance to think about. Normally, things like the roof, windows, balcony, and common elements would all be taken care of with these fees.

Plus, there is no grass to cut, flower beds to weed, or bushes to trim. Overall, there is much less maintenance with condos, so it can create a more 'hands-off' investment.

We think condos can be great, but like any other investment, run the numbers to make sure they look good.

When evaluating condominiums, be aware that the monthly fees can change. Sometimes you may be exposed to large increases in your monthly carrying costs. Be sure to have your lawyer review the condominium documents before finalizing the purchase to gauge your exposure to these types of situations.

Question 3 – I am a bit of a handy guy and can do a lot of work myself. I think I would like to buy a beat-up place to fix up and wanted to get your thoughts?

This is a really common question, which there really isn't

one answer to.

The answer will change depending on your long-term vision and the amount of time you have to spare.

The one thing you can almost always count on is that the repairs will be more time consuming and costly than first expected. Unfortunately, we have learned that very well from experience.

There are a couple ways to look at this.

Fix and Sell – There are many variables that are out of your control when you are trying to fix up a property to sell immediately. We have to worry about things like market fluctuations, financing changes, unexpected repairs, time for permits, etc.

This can cause migraines in even the most experienced investors, and often the profit at the end of the day can be limited, especially when you factor in your time.

Fix and Rent - This approach is generally more appealing because you will get additional benefits from the work.

The same challenges can present themselves while doing repairs, but the outcome is a bit more pre-determined as you can typically get an idea of market rents before the purchase.

The added benefit is that you have a renovated home that looks good, which increases demand. You will have more equity in the home because the thought is that you have increased its value, and you will benefit from the appreciation on a more valuable home over the long run.

The second approach has more long-term benefits, but like

so many other topics with investing, it will come down to the numbers.

Example: If you could buy a home for $400,000 that needs $50,000 worth of work to bring its value up to $600,000, or you could buy a fully renovated home for $600,000, which one would suit you better?

Yes, with the first home you will have created an extra $150,000 in home equity. But you would have had to put a down payment on the home plus another $50,000 for renovations.

With the second example, you would only need to pay for a down payment out of your own pocket. It would be slightly larger, but overall, the acquisition of this investment property would use less of your own money out of the gates.

In each scenario, there are benefits and downfalls, so it truly is a personal choice.

We feel that if we can purchase a house with the work done it frees us up to move on to other investment and business opportunities, so you know which option we like.

Question #4 – I am in an area of strong appreciation and am interested in rental properties. Many of them look like they will be slightly negative cash flow but in the long run I think it will still work out because of the appreciation. Does this make sense?

This thinking is good...in a way.

The best thing about it is that you are looking at real estate as a long-term investment, which is key.

Real wealth in real estate comes from long-term investing.

Having someone pay you rent every month gives you access to the appreciation in the home, and they will pay down the mortgage every month. Plus, real estate acts as a good protection against inflation over the long run.

That's Rock Star stuff!

The whole 'negative cash flow' thing is a bit scary, here's why.

Appreciation is never guaranteed. The market can change and drop and it may take a few years to come back to where it was. Yes, those chances are much smaller if you are buying in the right areas, but the risk still exists.

Positive monthly cash flow is what carries you through the ups and downs. It is the foundation to build a diversified portfolio.

If you have multiple properties that are all negative by $100 a month, your monthly cash flow drops with each purchase. And if there is a vacancy, it's hit even harder.

But if you focus on positive cash flow you are building a stronger financial position for yourself with each purchase. Plus, if a vacancy comes up, the money coming in from the other properties can help cover the cost.

Ultimately, positive cash flow investing is always the way to go. If you decide to make a concession for some reason, maybe you get a great price, make sure you monitor it closely because negative cash flowing real estate can be a slippery slope.

Question #5 – What about investing in new homes

purchased from a builder?

Great question!

There are a lot of new home opportunities available, with high-end finishes like granite countertops or appliances used as bonuses.

Buying new, like anything else, has both up and downs.

The two most appealing factors are the lack of repairs that will be needed for the home and the price.

There is very little work to be done to a new home to get it ready to rent out because...well, it's all new! It will also limit any maintenance calls that you may get because things should be in good working order and much of it will be covered under warranty from the builder.

Often homes being sold from a builder off of floor plans will have an elevated value when the home is finally built. This can create a chance to have some equity in the home from the time you take ownership.

But like any other investment, the equity is not guaranteed.

Typically, new homes are completed about two years after they go on sale. There are a lot of things that can happen in two years.

A good example is the market meltdown in the US a few years back. If you had purchased a home prior to the correction, you were still expected to pay way above market value for the home or risk losing your deposit.

The one big thing that investing in new homes does not have is <u>control</u>.

We've already covered that most successful investors have built wealth through controlling their investments. Buying a new home takes some of that control away from us.

Essentially, what we are doing is handing over our money to someone else until the home is completed, with no control until then.

There are definitely worse situations to be in, but it is something we need to be aware of.

Also, we should take into account the lost opportunity that parting with that money represents.

Often, builders will require larger down payments than resale transactions.

For instance, if we were buying a $600,000 from a builder, it is realistic for them to ask us for about $100,000 as a down payment. This is money that we will not be able to invest elsewhere now.

Another view is that we could take $80,000 of that $100,000 and buy a $400,000 home with 20% down. We would still have $20,000 left over and our investment would be generating positive cash flow much sooner than the new home, which is not even built yet!

So, our money could be working for us faster.

Who knows, maybe we take the extra $20,000 plus the cash flow over the next two years and buy a second home. Now we have two homes making us money instead of one.

Whatever the investment is, it is important to look at both sides of the coin because for every opportunity that you jump on, you may have to give up another one.

The good news is there are so many opportunities out there waiting for you that you will never be short!

Interesting Question #1 – As a retiree with only Old Age Security, is it possible to obtain a mortgage for a rental property?

This question does not only apply to retirees but the many people who are looking to invest on fixed incomes, disability payments being another example.

The best answer would come from a qualified investment mortgage broker in your area. But we can tell you what we have seen.

We have personally worked with investors on fixed incomes who have purchased **multiple** investment properties.

Sometimes down payments will need to be adjusted based on your income and credit score, but it is uncommon for it to be outright impossible.

There are many factors involved, which is why a great mortgage broker is an important part of every investment team.

The short answer is that we have seen people still invest and qualify for mortgages on fixed incomes, but because of the wide range of requirements, the details will be on a case by case scenario.

Chapter 11

Using Rock Star Marketing Systems to Fill Your Property – Part 1

The marketing tactics and tools that we covered in Chapter 4 apply directly to us today. In fact, we will break it down the same way. This should look familiar.

> L – <u>LEADS</u> for your properties
> A – <u>APPOINTMENTS</u> for your properties
> A – <u>APPLICATIONS</u> to rent your properties
> P – <u>PROFIT</u> from your properties

But now we want to get into a bit of the specifics around each section.

Let's not forget that a marketing system is an investor's best friend. That piece of the puzzle doesn't change one bit.

But that system will change slightly with each type of investment you have.

Let's get started.

1. <u>Leads</u> for your properties.

We have covered the key advertising methods to use when

trying to fill a property. But the ad you run for your rental property can have a big impact on the results.

Take a look at this ad from a local paper.

"SEMI for rent, 3 bedrooms, 3 baths, Central Air, close to schools, and shopping. $1,650/mo. Plus utilities. Call XXX-XXXX"

This is a typical ad that you would see advertising a property. It is typical because it is just like every other ad around it in the paper.

It has the number of bedrooms, the number of bathrooms, maybe one feature, the price, and the phone number.

Advertising your property is one thing, but advertising it effectively is another game altogether.

When you first advertise a rental property, you should only have a single goal in mind.

Get people to respond to your ad.

That's it!

Resist the urge to get ahead of yourself and focus on this one step.

A properly structured ad will increase the number of prospects that reach out to you (phone or email) for more information. This is the **only** goal of your ad.

Generally, the success of an ad is based on the cost per lead (CPL) that it generates.

Here is how to understand CPL.

Let's pretend we run two ads in two different newspapers for our rental home.

Ad 1 cost $200 and generated 15 calls.

Ad 2 cost $150 and generated 13 calls.

To calculate our CPL, we divide the cost of the ad by the number of leads (phone calls in this case) we receive.

Ad 1 200/15 equals a CPL of $13.33

Ad 2 150/13 equals a CPL of $11.53

In this example, each telephone call from a prospect costs us less with ad number 2. These numbers are close, but sometimes there is a large margin.

These numbers are important for us to watch because it allows us to determine where to spend our advertising budget.

We may want to spend a bit more money on the newspaper we used for Ad 2, to see if we can generate a few more calls for a lower price.

Cost Per Lead is not the only thing to consider.

Here is another example:

Ad 1 has a CPL of $20

Ad 2 has a CPL of $10

> But the difference between the people responding to the ads is large as well.
>
> In this case, only 2 people that called in from Ad 2 can afford the monthly rent. But 8 people that called in from ad 1 can afford the monthly rent.
>
> We are not as interested in people that can't afford the house we are advertising so Ad 1 is more attractive even with a higher cost per lead, because it attracted more people that could pay the monthly rent on our home.

That is a quick "marketing 101" lesson.

It is the type of information that too many investors overlook. It is not exciting to track every single lead that comes in by its source. But, it is a good way to make you a savvy investor.

It may take you some time to develop your own tracking system, but usually, a simple Microsoft Excel spreadsheet works fine. Sometimes we just keep a notepad with the details of each person that responded to our advertising.

It's not rocket science, so keeping it simple is probably best.

OK, so now that we covered a quick marketing lesson, we are back to the standard ad we looked at earlier.

Here it is again.

"SEMI for rent, 3 bedrooms, 3 baths, Central Air, close to schools, and shopping. $1,650/mo. Plus utilities. Call XXX-XXXX"

It is B-O-R-I-N-G!

If the goal of the ad is to get people to call us we want to stand out from the crowd a bit.

If our ad is similar to every other one, we are relying on chance to catch the reader's eye. Let's increase our chances!

The best way to entice a person to reach out to us is to paint a picture with words. We want to have people visualizing the home before they even see it.

> Describing unique features and standing out from the crowd are the keys to a good ad.

Here is an example of an ad we have placed in the past.

"IMMACULATE home on the North side. Huge deck, gleaming hardwood floors, 3 bedrooms, large bright kitchen, professionally finished basement, move right in, XXX-XXX-XXXX, 24hr msg"

(We're old, and while we originally used this ad in a newspaper, the same principles can be used online!)

There is a lot to this ad so let's break it down piece by piece to make sure we don't forget any parts.

"IMMACULATE home on the North Side"

There are two points that we are trying to get across with this portion of the ad. The first is that we want to make sure that people know the home is in good condition so we use "Immaculate."

This could be replaced with beautiful, perfect, gorgeous, etc.

The majority of rental properties are a bit run down because many landlords won't make minor repairs. This causes renters to lower their expectations a bit. If we can communicate to them that our home is in great condition, it is a plus for us.

We also make mention of the "North Side" is this particular ad. The reason is because this is a better area of the city. There is more demand for properties in this area from the quality of tenants we are looking for, so we want to call it out right away.

"Huge deck, gleaming hardwood floors"

Our goal here is to start creating a picture in the reader's mind. We could have put 'deck, hardwood' instead, but adding the descriptive words helps people visualize what you are talking about.

Which one would sound more appealing to you? We hope you thought it was the one we used.

This is the part of the ad where you want to call out the **unique advantages** your home has.

Adding the descriptive words may make the ad cost a bit more, but it is minimal.

Many investors look at advertising as an expense instead of an investment.

If you are placing an ad and the classified rep tells you the rate for the standard 2 or 3-line ad, don't be afraid to go over the word limit.

It will all come down to cost per lead and the quality of prospect you are attracting.

"3 bedrooms, large bright kitchen, professionally finished basement"

This is where we are describing the basics of the home. The number of bedrooms and if the home has a finished basement are the two most common questions we receive.

The finished basement is a selling feature so we definitely want to include it. Notice that we have used descriptive words (large, bright, professionally) for the kitchen and the basement.

This is helping us continue to paint a picture for people looking at the ad.

"Move Right In"

There is no science to this bit other than we feel that this helps to communicate that the home is in good condition and that it does not require any repairs.

"XXX-XXX-XXXX, 24hr msg"

This is a biggie!!

By offering a 24-hour message we are making it less threatening for the prospect to call about our home.

They don't feel like they are going to get a pushy person on the phone trying to 'sell' them on the property. Also, they can call anytime. Often, we will get calls late at night with this in our ad, which makes us happy our phone isn't ringing at that time!

The other benefit is that you won't be trying to take calls about your property while you are in an inconvenient situation such as checking out at the grocery store.

Yes, that really happens.

And when you are speaking to a cashier, with one hand in your wallet, and holding your phone to your ear, it can sometimes be hard to try to book an appointment with a prospective tenant. It will also make it really hard to track which ad the lead is coming from so that you can accurately track which ads are working best for you.

The downside with a 24-hour message is that you will have to follow up with people after they leave a message. This means you may get their voicemail, or you will have to call multiple times.

If you can handle the downside of using a 24-hour message, then it is probably the way to go.

Let's take a final look at the ads side by side to see the differences.

The 'Standard' Ad

"SEMI for rent, 3 bedrooms, 3 baths, Central Air, close to schools, and shopping. $1,650/mo. Plus utilities. Call XXX-XXXX"

The 'Rock Star' Ad

"IMMACULATE home on the North side. Huge deck, gleaming hardwood floors, 3 bedrooms, large bright kitchen, professionally finished basement, move right in, XXX-XXX-XXXX, 24hr msg"

We have had much more success using the Rock Star ad.

You may have noticed that we didn't include the monthly rent in our ad. This is done for a reason too.

That probably doesn't surprise you!

Including the monthly rent in the ad screens out potential tenants before you get the chance to speak with them.

Never forget the key to running ads.

> A properly structured ad will increase the number of prospects that reach out to you (phone or email) for more information. This is the **only** goal of your ad.

We want to make our phone ring.

By not including the rent in the ad, we will generate more calls. But because of this, some of the people calling may not be able to afford our property. So, we may have to deal with more people, but anyone who can't afford our home will be filtered out through the rest of the process.

Another reason we don't include the rent is because we are **always** open to negotiation.

For example, if we are asking for $1,650 a month in rent and we feel that we have found a perfectly suited tenant that can only afford $1,600, we may give the house to them.

If we had included the higher rent amount in the ad there is a good chance they would have never called us!

OK, now that we have gotten the text of the ad covered, there is one other tactic we use.

Have you ever seen things like these in your local classified section?

- Heading Text
- Picture
- Coloured Text
- Reverse Coloured Text (colour background with white font)

Adding additional features like this to your ad will help it to stand out.

Depending on your paper, it may only be a few extra dollars to have one of these options.

Typically, the picture option is the most expensive so you may want to try others, but always ask what type of specials or packages the paper has.

We once found out we could get a picture in the paper once a week for no additional cost just by asking.

If you look at a classified page in your local paper, you will notice that your eyes are more drawn to the ads with these features, and if you get more eyes on your ads, you should get more calls as well.

Like anything else, with advertising your property it is good to test it and track it to see if it is working.

As you can tell, it is important to put some thought into your ads and we have only covered newspaper ads.

Chapter 11's Assignment

Go online. Check out Kijiji and Craigslist and take a look at the real estate rental sections. See what stands out to you and decide how you can do the same for your ad. Then write an ad using some Rock Star principles. If you don't have a rental property yet, write it for your own home.

Don't forget to use descriptive words to paint a picture in the reader's head. Ask someone to read a regular online classified ad (i.e. Kijiji) and then yours to get some feedback.

Chapter 12

Using Rock Star Marketing Systems to Fill Your Properties – Part 2

Remember our marketing system for our properties? Just in case you forgot, here it is one more time.

      L – LEADS for your properties
      A – APPOINTMENTS for your properties
      A – APPLICATIONS to rent your properties
      P – PROFIT from your properties

Leads for your properties are so important that we are going to continue to focus on ways to generate them today.

All the steps above are big keys to successful investing, but without leads, you will never get to work on the next steps.

Makes sense, right?

Now that we have covered our newspaper ads we need to understand what the differences are when we advertise on the Internet.

In Chapter 4 we covered many of the different websites we can advertise on. Usually, each city will have some local ones as well that you can use.

Now, we want to continue to focus on the ads that we place.

The great thing about advertising on the Internet is it usually gives us a better opportunity to "sell" our property because we don't have as many limits put on our ad.

Our goal for the ad does not change at all, but now we have some new tactics to use.

> A properly structured ad will increase the number of prospects that reach out to you (phone or email) for more information. This is the **only** goal of your ad.

A huge benefit of online advertising is being able to include some great pictures of your home.

With text ads, we are forced to try and paint a picture in the reader's mind using only words. Here, we can put the exact picture we want them to have with the ad.

It is important to use a picture that makes the home look good.

The picture alone can change the number of people that will view your ad.

It is almost always better to use a picture in your ad (unless it is an ugly looking property), but it is best to use a stunning photo of your home.

Here's an example of an excellent headline:

GORGEOUS TWO STOREY HOME IN AUBURN BAY BUILT IN 2008

Even though we use an actual picture in most of our online

advertising, it is still important to try to paint a picture in the tenant's mind with the words we use.

With this headline, you already get a sense of the home because it is 'Gorgeous' and it is relatively new since the year it was built is in the headline. Plus, this ad uses the area as a selling feature as well.

This is some good stuff! Now, look at this headline...

House for Rent Taradale NE

This is a great example of a typical, boring headline. Just from these two headlines, we would be much more interested in the first ad. Especially since both homes are listed for rent at the **exact same price.**

We can tell from Kijiji that both these ads were posted within minutes of each other. We can also see how many visits each ad has received since they were posted.

The first ad with the long headline had 49 visits. The second ad with the short headline had 31 visits.

That's a HUGE difference for two ads, side by side, listed at the same price.

That means the first ad received **58% more** views.

Here are the full ads side by side...

 GORGEOUS TWO STOREY HOME IN AUBURN BAY BUILT IN 2008 $1,750.00
GORGEOUS TWO STOREY HOME IN AUBURN BAY BUILT IN 2008 (About 1 year Old) Totally upgraded home in the lake community of Auburn Bay Two storey, 3 bedroom, bonus room, double attached garage, 2.5 bath, ...

 House for Rent Taradale NE $1,750.00
House for Rent Taradale NE Beautiful 2 storey home in Taradale NE Calgary, only a 10 minute drive to Sunridge, Calgary fenced yard perfect for families or for entertaining around the firepit for

Hopefully, you are starting to see the difference good advertising can make.

There are a couple of final tips for online advertising.

Length of Ad – If you have space, and it doesn't cost you anything extra, use it! Be as descriptive as possible, list the features, explain the benefits, and tell a story.

We once had a property with a pear tree in the backyard and used that in our advertising. People actually came to the house and asked where the pear tree was.

The pear tree didn't add value to the home, but it made the home stand out in people's minds, which was the ultimate goal.

Methods of Contact – Give people multiple ways to contact you. Most people looking online will email you any questions they have. But, some people viewing your ad may want more information quickly and may try you by phone.

People will prefer to respond to you in different ways, so give them options.

Pricing – Test your ad with and without pricing (remember, it is free to test on many online classified sites). Keep in mind that you may be pre-qualifying people to early in the process if you include pricing in your ad. You may want to leave it blank to see if you can generate more leads and then qualify them at that point.

Updates – Over time you may want to update your ad to give it a fresh look. Because people can see the date it was posted online, it can sometimes give the impression that the home is not desirable even if it has only been there for a couple of weeks.

In cases like this, we may delete our first ad before putting up a new one. We would change the headline and the picture used with the ad.

If we used a picture of the front of the house, we may use a picture of the nicest room or feature of the home in the updated ad.

Pictures – If you are going to use interior pictures, be sure to turn on ALL the lights before taking them. You want to use bright, vibrant pictures and the lighting helps a lot.

Also, take the time to make sure they look OK once they are uploaded to the website. Sometimes your pictures may get distorted when they're put online. Try to take the necessary steps to fix this.

Appointments for your properties — By far, the most important way to show your property is to try and show multiple people at once.

We covered this in chapter 4 and we personally do this with every property we own.

But there are some other techniques you can use to try to increase the number of people that come out to your home.

Just like our reason for advertising, when we respond to voicemails or emails from prospective tenants there is only one goal in mind.

> The **only** goal to have when speaking to prospective tenants is to get them to meet you at the property for a viewing.

No matter how hard you try you can never do a home

justice by explaining it over the phone or by email.

People will contact you with a range of questions. You will want to answer these questions, but try to guide the tenant to the house at the same time.

Here is a common scenario.

Question: "What type of area is it in? Is it close to a nice school for my kids?"

Response: "<<Answer the question>>. You know what? The best way to see what I am talking about is to come take a look at the place and see if you even like it and then from there I can show you all the details of the area.

I am available on _____ at _____ PM. Does that work for you?"

Did you notice that the only intention was to get the person out to the home? It wouldn't have mattered what the question was, the goal would still be to get them out to see if they like it.

We will always answer their questions and try to give them the information they are looking for. But, no matter how much explaining you do, it is always better for someone to see the house in person. There are two reasons:

1 – To visually decide if the home fits their needs. If it does, they will start to become emotionally attached to it.

2 – To allow you to build a relationship with the tenant.

Many investors forget about number 2.

They don't realize that building relationships is the key to being a good landlord and it starts from the first time you meet the tenant.

Applications **to rent your properties** — Once the tenants (remember, the goal is to set multiple appointments for the same time) show up to the property, the relationship building begins.

We will welcome each tenant into the home and tell them to feel free to show themselves around.

Whenever you are showing your property, be sure to turn on ALL the lights, even if it is a beautiful, sunny day outside.

Open windows, turn on ceiling fans and pick up and papers left on the front porch.

Try to arrive 15 minutes before your appointments to do this before people start wandering through your home.

It seems like really small stuff, but these are the little steps that will separate you from other landlords.

Our goal is to give them the freedom to look around, get a feel for the place, and speak to each other, without anyone looking over their shoulder.

This will help achieve the single goal we are striving for at this part of the process.

> When showing a property, **all** we are trying to do is generate applications. If needed, we can qualify them afterwards.

Typically, after people are done looking through the home, they will end up in the kitchen.

Just like most dinner parties, no matter how big or small the home, people end up in the kitchen.

This is the time to start getting some feedback on the home and also to understand why the tenants are looking for a new place to live.

Often, the most valuable information you can get as a landlord is the reason why people are looking for a home. Usually, this opens up a whole can of worms.

Not too many people enjoy moving, so it is a fairly safe bet that they aren't looking for a new place just for fun.

If your home fits as a good solution to the reason the tenant is moving, then your chances of them renting it are much greater.

Renting out a property isn't just a matter of showing up and keeping your fingers crossed. It is about trying to fulfil the needs of the people you are renting to.

Once you find out what their needs are, it is your chance to explain how your property fits these needs. This is your chance to "sell" your home.

It is a much more effective way than to follow them around room by room explaining why you think your home is great.

It will also allow you to build a stronger relationship with your tenant.

Chapter 13

Tips on Closing and Managing the Deal

The information we go through today isn't taught in any real estate investing course. These are all from real-world trial and error.

Yes, there are always some errors.

Over time, any real estate investor has their unique way of doing things but all the successful ones we've spoken with use the same tactics we are going to cover.

The 5 Most Common Ways Investors Self Sabotage Themselves

Once you have selected the lucky person that gets to move into your house, there are still a few things that need to be done before you can take a step back and start to put the property on autopilot.

Like so many other projects and tasks we undertake, it is that final push to the finish that can make or break all the work put in to get to that point. Not taking care of the details at the end would be like replacing a spare tire and not tightening the bolts.

Self-Sabotage #1 - Not Preparing and Reviewing the Leases

The title says it all, right?

That's exactly why it is taken for granted because it seems so simple.

The meeting to sign the leases starts off the official landlord/tenant relationship. It is important to come across as someone who is organized and competent.
Showing up and then fumbling through papers is not usually the best way to kick things off.

The solution is easy. Prepare the paperwork beforehand. Make a copy for anyone that is going to be signing the lease and have all the correct information filled in (ex. name, address, rent amount, lease terms, etc.).

This takes you 10 minutes the night before and goes a long way to making the process smoother.

But **reviewing and understanding the leases** beforehand is even more important. Be sure you know what you are asking your tenant to sign because if you don't know, how can you expect them to?

You want to understand the language in your agreement so you can answer any questions that may come up and ensure that you give the information they need to sign off on the lease.

Again, this only takes a short time before your meeting and will help make the process much smoother.

We've gotten into the habit of reviewing the entire lease with the tenant point by point and explaining it in plain

English. Sometimes this can be a bit tedious but our experiences have shown us that the tenant is both appreciative and happy to have a complete understanding of what they are signing.

It also ensures they understand everything, so there are no discrepancies in the future as to who is responsible for specific items or tasks.

Self-Sabotage #2 – Making it all About Yourself

This is a biggie! If you're able to avoid this, it will definitely help your results.

Too many people just care about what is in it for themselves. They will meet with the tenants and only focus on what the tenants' responsibilities are. Things like paying rent, maintaining the property, and not having pets, would be the focus of the entire meeting.

Yes, these are all important points, but they aren't the only ones.

There are also important issues for the tenant, which need to be explained.

When explaining the terms of the tenancy, you want to make sure that the tenant understands they are getting value for the rent they are paying every month.

Some good examples of points to focus on for the tenant could be:

- The responsibility of the landlord to maintain the appliances.
- No worries about the furnace and A/C because it is our responsibility.

- Pointing out one or two good features of the home that they won't have to worry about because they are new.

We even use the same tactic when asking for post-dated cheques. We would say something like this.

"It probably makes sense to just have postdated cheques. That way you don't have to worry about tracking us down or mailing out a cheque every month, which would probably be a pain in the butt for you. What do you think?"

You can see that a casual conversation is fine but try to remember to explain how things benefit them. Here is what one investor has said in the past:

"You should provide me with postdated cheques because if something happens and I don't have the rent on the 1st of the month there could be problems because I have a mortgage payment to make."

That is an actual quote from an investor. And the tenant's entire body language became more negative after that was said.

In the second example, it was all about the investor. Do not follow the second example!

You are building and starting a relationship here, show that you care.

Self-Sabotage #3 – Not Preparing the Property for Move In

Let's face it. Anyone that has just filled a vacant property is happy.

The tendency is to sit back a bit and wait for the tenant to move in. Sometimes that can be 4-6 weeks away, maybe even longer. A lot can happen in the time, like cobwebs, grass growing, and uncollected newspapers.

If you want a guarantee that your tenants are let down when they move in, then this is a sure-fire way to do it.

Instead, we can use this time to "**wow**" the tenants, and it's easy! All you have to do is maintain a vacant property.

Take the time to cut the grass, shovel the driveway, and collect the mail.

And if you want to take things to the next level, you can get some planters for the front porch, put a gift basket in the home, or make a snowman for their arrival. Yes, a snowman.

Remember, make it about them. If you were moving into a new home and things like this were done for you, how would you feel?

If you stop maintaining the place between the time the leases are signed and the tenant moves in, you are likely getting off to a bad start!

Self-Sabotage #4 – Ignoring Early Requests

Whenever someone moves into a new home, there are bound to be things that are discovered that need some attention.

It could be a broken phone jack, a loose door handle, or a slowly dripping faucet, but the chances of some small things coming up are very good.

This isn't specific to rental properties, it applies to any home.

Expecting to take a few calls during the first week or two after the tenant moves is realistic. It is always a nice surprise when it doesn't happen, but that is not typical.

Some landlords fall off the map here.

It is important to be responsive to the calls and help them through it. This might be the first time these people have ever lived outside of an apartment building so they may not know what to do.

Just because they are calling you, it doesn't mean there is a problem, they are looking for help. Most often, you can help them rectify the situation by explaining what to do.

One of our tenants was not sure how to go about running a new cable jack to the bedroom for her TV. There was nothing to be done, other than walking her through the process of getting the cable installed by the cable company.

She didn't even know the name of the cable company in the area. As a general rule, it can be good to be extra responsive to tenant phone calls or emails at the beginning of the lease.

Self-Sabotage #5 – Not Being Negotiable

Yes, rules are rules and as a landlord, we walk a fine line between enforcing them and building a relationship with our tenant.

It is important to run things as a business and follow the expectations and obligations that were outlined.

But…there is always a "but" …sometimes you have to use your own judgment to take care of certain situations.

Here's an example…

We had a bit a sewage backup about two weeks after a new tenant moved in. Generally, our tenants are responsible for the cost of repairing this, if it is done by their actions.

But in this case, we called a contractor and covered the cost before we knew if it was something the tenant did or not.

Before we got it fixed, we explained to the tenant that this is normally something they would take care of if it were caused by their negligence, but this time we will handle it for them because it was so close to the move in date.

We didn't want them to think that we will always take care of everything, but we also didn't want them thinking they moved into a dump.

This thought process comes from speaking to other tenants from many properties, some that we own and some that we don't. From speaking with them, we learned that they often felt taken advantage of in similar situations that were handled differently.

Rules are there for a reason and the lease is there to hold everyone accountable.

However, we have found not thinking about the lease and just thinking about what is fair to everyone involved often make the best decisions.

The same tenant from this example actually had another

backup about 2 years later. They actually brought up the first incident and gladly paid for the repair this time around.

The relationship that was built paid off.

If you lump all the above lessons together it is an easy way to self-sabotage your rental property, and we have seen it many times.

The key is to always remember there are two people that are involved in every rental agreement, and try to look at things from the other side as well.

Once you have all the kinks ironed out, it is time to go into property management mode and put your home on autopilot.

Here are some tips to help make the process smooth.

Property Management Tip #1 – Automate Rent

Rent is definitely an important part of a rental property, and ensuring it is in the bank on time is essential.

There are a couple options to make rent collection easier.

Post Dated Cheques – This is definitely the most common way of collecting rent. This puts you in control of depositing the rent. No phone calls or meetings, just grab the cheque for the month and head to the bank. (You can't demand them in all provinces but you can ask.)

Email Transfer – Almost anyone that uses online banking has access to email money transfers. Your tenant can set up a payment plan that will automatically email you money over on the due date every month. It is nice to open your email and see large sums of money waiting!

Pre-Authorized Payment Plan – Check with your bank to confirm the process of setting this up. This is similar to how your mortgage is paid: it comes out of a bank account automatically. You can set up a payment plan to have money transferred from your tenant's account to yours each month. One benefit of this over cheques is that you don't have to wait for them to clear; you will have access to the money right away.

Property Management Tip #2 – Don't Buy into Drama

As you build your portfolio of rental properties and deal with more tenants, you are going to hear some unbelievable stories.

And what is even more unbelievable is that some of them will be true!

One tenant that we had worked with had moved into a house with his girlfriend because they were having a child and they needed more room.

Two months later, he found out that he was not the father and decided to move out. The mother had to move too because she could not afford the home on her own.

Yes, it sounds like a Jerry Springer episode, and in cases like these, there is not much you can do.

But in situations of late rent, you **cannot** fall for "the rent is coming" stories.

However, you can work with the tenant to come up with a payment plan but as soon as they break their word you will need to hold them accountable immediately. If you start feeling sorry for them because of the story they are telling, you are running the risk of letting them stay in the house without paying.

And if they don't pay, guess who does?

You do.

You are bound to come across some unfortunate circumstances, but ultimately paying the rent is a business transaction and has to be treated as one.

Property Management Tip #3 – Jumping to Conclusions

This is going to sound like the opposite of tip #2 but it goes back to walking that 'landlord line' of building a relationship while running a business.

Some investors will start an eviction process the day after they have not received the rent, without speaking with the tenant.

In most cases, the disadvantages of damaging the relationship will outweigh the advantages of starting the eviction process sooner.

Realistically, if you wait 2 or 3 days longer to try to evict someone, there is a slim chance that it will have a serious negative impact on you.

But there is a reason for this, and that is to try and communicate with the tenant.

Keeping open lines of communication is the most important thing you can do. This way you know what the situation is.

While at an old employer, we had a payroll malfunction at the end of the month and my (Nick) pay was delayed by a few days. The company offered letters to provide to banks and landlords in case any mortgage or rent payments were affected.

One of our tenants once left on vacation and didn't realize that we had run out of postdated cheques. We didn't hear from him for 3 days but he got payment over to us right away.

Situations like this are not common, but they do happen. We always take into account the past history of the tenant and try to reach out to them to understand the problem.

An investor we know got a call from a neighbour of his rental property telling him that police had been there. He overreacted and went to the property to see what kind of "illegal" things they were up to. He was surprised to learn that the tenants' son had been mugged so the police were called.

This is a perfect example where a bit of communication would have gone a long way because the manner in which he approached the tenant caused some frustration for the tenant and damaged their relationship.

Property Management Tip #4 – It's a Team Effort

Never forget that this is a two-way street -- the landlord/tenant relationship has to work both ways for it to be successful.

A tenant we had was in the middle of some employment problems recently, so their rent was late for 4 or 5 months straight. In fact, one month it was paid on the last day of the month instead of the 1st!

But there is a reason we let this happen. It is because every single time they said the rent, or part of it, would be paid on a certain day, it was. They consistently lived up to their word and kept us in the loop.

Because of this, we were more than happy to work with them and arrange a different payment schedule. In this example, we never filed eviction paperwork once.

And they must have thanked us 100 times for working with them during a difficult time.

Some landlords may disagree with this approach but as long as the tenant has been good, and kept their word, we are willing to work with them through many circumstances.

Property Management Tip #5 – Find Some Support

Surprisingly, it took us a while to learn that we weren't in this alone. There are a lot of landlord groups available to help out.

They provide a good chance to speak with other people that are managing properties.

It is amazing what little, itty-bitty, tips you can pick up that will help you along the way.

If you do an Internet search for local landlord associations, you will find some options. Most of the time the fees are minimal and the benefits are worth it.

If you have a chance to attend a meeting of the group you join, take advantage of it. You will probably discover local vendors and property managers with a ton of information to share.

Part 3:

Student Rentals

Chapter 14

Back to School with Student Rentals

Those who go first, discover so many things that benefit those who follow. Quite a few discoveries are learned "the hard way." Lewis and Clark had no maps to follow as they trail blazed the westward trail. They were the mapmakers!

Over the last few years, that's how it's felt to us with our Student Rental properties.

We definitely were not the first, but our network of investors did not include very many people (zero, actually) when we first started with student rentals.

We've learned a lot of things over the years and in this chapter, we're going to share the key points with you.

1. Lead with <u>income</u> on student rentals.

We've been tempted on many occasions to put an offer on a student rental property because of its close proximity to the school or the immaculate condition of the property.

But the single thing that has allowed us to always maximize profits has been a very specific focus on the income that the property can produce.

For example, a property that can physically have a maximum of 5 bedrooms is not as good as a property with 4 bedrooms with an unfinished basement. That unfinished basement may allow for 2 to 4 extra bedrooms.

Even if you don't have the funds to finish the basement immediately, the potential for increased income exists forever.

With a 5-bedroom house, you will never be able to increase the income in a big way. Of course, you can increase rents but you'll never be able to add a quick 25%-100% extra income.

Check out this example...

We have a property with 4 bedrooms and an unfinished basement. We're able to rent out those 4 bedrooms and start to create some cash flow, and at some point in time, we'll be able to add another 3 bedrooms to the large unfinished basement and increase our rent by 75%. However, we know someone who bought a 5-bedroom house with a crawl space instead of a full basement. So, they can never increase the income on that property (unless of course they apply for an addition and spend a considerable amount of money building it).

Something else to consider...

We purchased a 7-bedroom student rental that we purchased purely because of the size. The interior of the property had 30-year-old shag carpets, a garage leaning over on its foundation, a second kitchen in the basement that looked more like a wood workshop with a sink than a kitchen, and a bathroom that had exposed electrical wire next to an open shower.

However, it had large rooms and the overall house size was big. It was not fully rented, but we knew that with some basic improvements in flooring and paint and with our "Rock Star Marketing Skills," we could likely fill all the rooms quickly.

And we did.

And then over the years we slowly renovated both kitchens, both bathrooms, and even added a third shower in the house.

Now, the house is fully rented every year without fail and with relative ease. And it is cash flowing at almost $1,000 per month.

If we had chosen a house that looked a little nicer, but that had fewer bedrooms, it would never have allowed us to truly maximize our income potential.

So…

Always, always, always focus on what the maximum income potential of a student rental property is by comparing the size of the house/unit/condo to others in the area. It's not something that can be easily changed.

And the #1 reason you purchase a student rental property is for cash flow.

2. Focus on close proximity to the university/college.

One of the reasons we are able to rent out our properties very easily is because of their proximity to the school.

Here's an example…

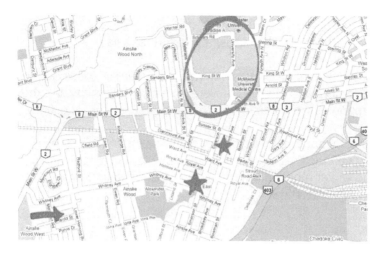

The large circle on the map is McMaster University. The two stars represent two of our properties. Notice how both are very close to the school.

And there's something else that may not be as obvious from this map. The one is on a main street that leads directly into the school. Under normal circumstances, you would likely not invest in a property on a main street.

A quiet street is more appealing after all. However, for student rentals, we have found that students love direct and easy access to school. This street even has a bus route. And for advertising purposes, it's a **gold mine.**

When we put a sign for rent on that property, we generate enough leads to fill that one and the other property, which is a little further away.

And we've actually filled other properties that our friends own from the leads generated by that close property.

The high visibility and exposure it has is a real asset.

Now, notice the little arrow a little further away.

We looked at properties out there that were in a little better condition, and the streets were actually a little nicer, but the properties were vacant.

And vacant properties do not generate income. On the above map that street may look close to the school, but in the winter months that distance is a 25-30-minute walk through the snow.

Not fun.

Students love convenience.

We took what we learned from this school and applied it to another university. There was an opportunity to buy a property on a main street leading into York University.

This was new construction and the builder was giving a discount for the property because of its location. We snapped it up immediately because we knew good exposure would mean that we could keep the rooms filled easily.

You see...

Some students will undoubtedly leave you in the middle of the school year. They will go to Europe to "find themselves" or "drop out" for no reason whatsoever.

So, you need to be prepared to fill a one-off vacant room. And the other students in the house usually do a good job of doing that for you if you've been fair to them. They'll want a friend or someone they know in the house over a complete stranger.

However, you may find yourself in a situation where you need to fill that room yourself. And that room may represent the difference between a positive cash flow property and a negative cash flow property. So, it's critical you get it done.

And when you have a property with high exposure to students walking, driving or taking the bus past the property – your chances of filling a single room mid-year increase dramatically!

We also purchased a student rental on the main street by York.

We've never had a problem filling any of the rooms in that property.

However, we have a friend who bought a slightly less expensive smaller property further away (only a few streets away).

He had such a difficult time filling that property that he had to accept months of vacancies and much less cash flow.

It became such a difficult process to get exposure on his property that a few years ago he sold it.

So…the lesson here?

Proximity to schools is a huge positive because students love being able to wake up and run to school in a couple of minutes. We've been told this countless times.

And, high exposure gives you a huge marketing advantage when creating leads for that property. You'll likely generate so many that other properties you may own in the area can be filled with students as well.

3. Keep your options open whenever possible.

Whenever possible we purchase properties with separate basement entrances. This gives us flexibility with our properties.

For example…

If we have a property with 5 bedrooms (main floor and 2nd floor) and 2 bedrooms in the basement … we prefer the basement to have a separate entrance if possible.

And for any properties with over 5 bedrooms, we try to have a second kitchen and full bathroom in the basement.

A separate basement entrance combined with a kitchen and full bathroom gives us the opportunity to have two different groups of people in the house.

It can sometimes be difficult to find a group of 7 students that know each other. It's much easier to find a group of 5.

And we prefer renting to groups because they seem to share responsibilities like cleaning and garbage duty better than those that don't know each other.

So, if we can divide the house into two "zones" we can rent out the main floor and upstairs to a group of 5 and the basement to a completely separate small group of 2.

We can even close off access to the basement from within the house and rent out the basement separately to a professor with a small family.

We've even paid extra for a property to have a new home builder properly build a basement entrance and have the zoning permits completed for it. That extra expense up front will give us years of options and flexibility with the property that we would not otherwise have.

Chapter 14's Assignment

If you're interested in student rental investing start booking appointments with a realtor to view some. Examine the income of each property closely and compare properties to each other. Don't be turned off by busy streets. Go visit the Off-Campus Housing Office in the college or university. That visit will be invaluable because you'll get an immediate feel for rental rates in the area and the preferred areas that the students like to rent in.

Chapter 15

Class #202 Advanced Student Rentals

If you find a property that generates a good amount of revenue and is close to the university or college, you'll want to check out if the current rent is above or below the average rent in the area.

That way, when the current students renting the property leave, you won't get an unwelcome revenue shock.

1. Always get an understanding of rent rates in the area.

You'll find rent is going to be dictated by some pretty obvious factors. Here are the main factors that influence rent prices:

- Proximity to school
- Access to things like pizza parlours/convenience stores/restaurants
- The condition of the property

Any student rental area is going to have other houses with "For Rent" signs in the windows. Call the number on a couple of the properties and ask the current landlords how much they are charging for rent.

We've even stopped in front of houses with students hanging out on the porches and just asked them how much they pay and what they get for that. Are things like utilities and Internet included or extra?

2. Get familiar with the Off-Campus Housing Department and any zoning bylaws in your area.

You can usually just drop by in person and you'll be amazed at how quickly you can get some research done.

For example, Mohawk College in Ontario has big glass covered cork boards located outside their office with different neighbourhoods broken out into "zones" and the average rental amounts for each area.

This is a quick way to figure out the revenue you'll be able to generate and how much competition you're facing.

Most universities and colleges have great online Off-Campus Housing resources as well. McMaster University in Hamilton, Ontario is a great example.

The site (macoffcampus.mcmaster.ca) has a ton of information for landlords.

And most importantly, these Off-Campus Housing websites are often the primary means for marketing your property. We'll be discussing more marketing strategies for student rentals in an upcoming lesson.

Off-Campus Housing will also have important zoning information for you to consider.

Many universities and cities have ZERO by-laws around student housing. For example, the University of Toronto and York University both have no bylaws for student rental properties (as we type this anyway – things can change, so it's important for you to check for yourself).

But the City of Waterloo, Ontario does.

Their Off-Campus Housing website has this on it:

Lodging house licenses

The City of Waterloo Lodging House Licensing By-Law requires that any property with 4 or more lodgers obtain a permit accompanied by a license number before listing. We will not list such a property without proof of license. You may contact the Waterloo Fire Prevention office at 519-884-0900 or check out the City of Waterloo Protective Services website for information regarding licensing and your accommodation.

So, in order for you to advertise your property on their website, you have to meet the By-Law requirements.

You'll want to investigate possible by-laws in your area prior to purchasing a property for student rental purposes.

You don't want to buy a nice single-family home only to find you can't rent it out to students because the city may be limiting the number of student rentals on your street.

If your area doesn't have by-laws, it's still an extremely good idea to call the local fire department and ask if they will do a walkthrough of your property. They'll check window sizes and exits and give you a good idea if you're property passes minimum city fire codes.

6. Insurance for Student Rental Properties.

Up until fairly recently, you could always find an insurance broker willing to insure student rental properties for approximately the same amount it would cost to insure a single-family home.

$600 per year or so.

Recently, it's becoming much more difficult to insure student rentals. We are currently paying as much as $2,800 on some properties and even to get that we had to call a dozen or so insurance companies.

Most of the larger companies, like State Farm or AllState, won't want anything to do with them. But don't get discouraged, keep calling around. Or ask your local investing group … insurers for these do exist. You just have to dig a little harder.

So, make sure you include this higher insurance amount into your cash flow calculations for the property.

As a little aside: We do know landlords who have "regular rental insurance" on their student rental properties.

We're not sure if that's to save costs, or they don't know the difference, but we definitely recommend getting the proper insurance for your property.

7. Managing Student Rental Properties.

Setting expectations with students early will be the best approach to management.

Sometimes these kids are leaving home for the very first time, so they don't know where to call for basic things like cable or Internet hook-up (if they're taking care of it themselves).

Other simple things, like where the breaker panel is or what day of the week the garbage goes out are things you'll have to cover with them at first.

But once they get into the swing of things, those types of calls quickly stop.

A good friend of ours puts together something he calls "the bible" for each of his properties.

And we use that approach for student rentals. It's a really good way to organize all of the important data for your student tenants.

We'll get a big bright red binder and inside include things like:

a) Local Phone Company information – so if the phones go down they can call them first.

b) Local Utilities and Gas Company details – so if something like the rented hot water tank stops working and they can't reach us they know who to call.

c) The Local Cable Company.

d) Pizza shops in the area! (You can also list grocery stores, banks, and other places in the area they may need/want to visit.)

e) The Garbage and Recycling Pick-up schedule.

f) If we're providing Internet service for them, we'll include the security key to access the network.

g) A list of house rules – around partying and any resulting damage, cleanliness of the kitchen and bathrooms.

h) Contact information for a local handyman.

i) A copy of their lease.

j) Any annual rent increases that we've agreed to.

k) Local bus routes and schedules.

l) If we're not managing the property, the contact information for the Property Manager.

m) If we don't have postdated cheques, we can list the process and dates of the month we'll be picking up rent cheques.

n) Anything else that's appropriate for that specific property

o) A list of things to avoid flushing down the toilet - this helps avoid sewage backups in older neighbourhoods!

By putting it all in one bright coloured binder, they seem to remember it better. So, whenever they call about something we ask, "did you check in the bright coloured binder?"

It may take a while, but eventually, it sinks in that everything they need is covered in there.

Also, we usually have one central corkboard in the house where any timely information can be shared. We'll usually have this in the kitchen or in the "common area," which is the area in the house used like a family or living room by the students.

That way, if there's been a change to the garbage schedule or rent collection, we can communicate it via email and on the corkboard.

Centralized point of contact.

We often centralize our communication with the students so that we use one email address for any emails to the group within the house.

And...

We'll have one phone number for any incoming calls to us. Over time, many of them have gotten a hold of our cell phone numbers, but if they call too much we explain that we prefer to keep our cell phones for emergencies, that way we know if they call it's important.

So, instead of calling us for things like a fridge or washing machine repair, we suggest that they just fire off an email instead – usually everyone prefers that and we've never had an issue with it.

A little tip for you...

We have one specific property, that for whatever reason the students in it constantly locked themselves out of their room.

We used to make a 30-minute drive up to the house each time this would happen.

We finally had the bright idea to buy a key lockbox from Home Depot (like the ones realtors use on the front door of a house) and put extra keys for each room in it.

We then find a secure location for it, a handrail or a garage perhaps. That way when we get students who are locked out of their room, we direct them to the lockbox and give them the code for it.

That saves us a long drive and the next time we're at the property we change the code so that the lockbox is secure again.

What about yard work on the property, small maintenance jobs, and the appliances?

Because student rentals are often surrounded by many other student rentals, you'll usually find someone in the area who is cutting grass and trimming bushes for a reasonable rate.

With a little searching around the neighbourhood, we've always managed to find a retired man or woman looking for a little extra work. On one property, we found a young boy looking to make some cash.

They'll usually take care of the lawn for a very reasonable rate.

And we've managed to find retired professionals looking for small handyman jobs as well. These contacts are perfect for the odd piece of broken glass, loose door handle, or leaky faucet.

If you don't see any signs for such services in the area check www.Kijiji.ca and you'll quickly have a list of people to call. Search for "local handyman" in your area.

If you're using older used appliances, do a quick search on www.YellowPages.ca in your area for used appliances, and you'll quickly find several.

Most used appliance stores do on-site service for a small fee. We've had fridges fixed for $100 that have lasted for years afterwards. That has saved us $200 or $300. It may not sound like a lot but when dealing with multiple properties, these costs can quickly add up and you need to control them.

If you end up needing to replace an appliance, these stores will often deliver a "new" used appliance and haul out the old one for you. You won't have to go to the property and handle this, they'll do it all for you.

We just let the students know what is going on and often have the used appliance store co-ordinate delivery times directly with the students at the house.

Chapter 15's Assignment

If you're thinking about investing in student rentals, start driving by the areas you're interested in and call some landlords. Ask them how much they're charging for each room in the house. Next, visit the Off-Campus Housing Department of the University or College either in person or online. Investigate possible local city by-laws that may apply to your student rental property.

Chapter 16

<u>Attracting Students to Your Property</u>

Whether you already own one or more student rental properties, or you're planning on investing in one shortly, one thing that's on every investor's mind is simple...

Getting Students into your properties!

The truth of the matter is this: once you have a system for attracting students into your properties, you gain an incredible amount of confidence about investing.

You'll use similar steps whether you need to fill an entire house with 7 bedrooms or if you're just "backfilling" a single room.

We want to quickly go over a very simple plan for getting students into your properties

Step 1: Getting the Word Out That You Have Rooms Available

Student rentals are a little different than other properties.

Instead of using the general advertising resources that you may normally use, the absolute best way to generate leads is going to be the Off-Campus Housing Department's website.

#1 Resource: off-campus housing department will be your best resource for student tenants.

Normally, during their first year of study at a college or university, students will pay to stay in the residences provided by the school.

Many are coming from out of town, they haven't made friends yet ... so it's safer and more convenient for them to stay in the "official" residences of the school.

What we've found is that towards the middle or end of their first year, groups of students will begin banding together to look for a place of "their own" to stay in.

They want the freedom of living "off campus."

That's where you come in – offering your properties for rent.

One of the main resources that students have available to them are the postings at the Off-Campus Housing Department.

Depending on the university or college these postings will be "offline" (meaning on a bulletin board in front of the office), "online" (on a website), or both.

A quick visit to the Off-Campus Housing website for the school close to your property will give you an idea of what they offer.

Here's what's available at the University of British Columbia's Off-Campus Housing department:

Finding a place

There are many ways to search for an apartment in Vancouver—from websites to notice boards.

At UBC:
Student Union Building, basement level
Graduate Student Society, Thea Koerner House, main floor foyer

Other sources:

- Rentsline
- Craigslist
- Renthello
- PadMapper
- ESLRENT.com (international students)
- Vancouver Apartment Rentals
- My Ideal Home Rentals
- Rentseeker.ca
- Search4StudentHousing.com

We don't have a property in British Columbia, but in a matter of seconds with a quick Google search, we found this information. And the reason we're doing this at a school where we ourselves don't own property is to show you how easy it is to dig up this type of information.

But don't stop at just reviewing what you find online. Make sure you make a trip into the Off-Campus Housing department's office.

A quick 5-minute chat with the person behind the desk can give you great insight into the areas that the students prefer and the rent rates.

Don't leave without that information.

But a word of caution…

When we first purchased a student property by a new school we took a little trip over to the Off-Campus Housing office.

The person behind the desk proceeded to tell us "how crazy new landlords were getting because they were asking $600 a month per room!"

She went on to explain that, "some people are just greedy."

Now…

What she didn't realize is that we just happened to be one of the new landlords planning on asking that much per room.

And what she also didn't realize was that because the new homes they were building in the area were so expensive, without asking for $600 per month, the properties would not produce income.

They would produce losses.

And with the money we were spending in finishing the basement of the property – even with the positive cash flow, we would not see a real return on our money for a couple of years.

Needless to say, her attitude about rent put some fear into us, but we pushed forward because…

We had two things working for us:

1. Our property was much closer to the university than the existing student rental properties (because this was a new construction on a plot of land previously undeveloped). Existing properties were 60 years old and two or three times further away from the school.

2. Our property was in tip-top-condition (because it was new) and to maximize our revenue we finished

the basement and we did it beautifully. We included a great IKEA kitchen, halogen lights, a full bathroom, an extra laundry room, new ceramic, and bright paint colours.

And we did go on to achieve our target of $600 per room.

What's the lesson?

Although Off-Campus Housing is a great resource for you – it's <u>you</u> who is the investor and ultimately has to make decisions about your properties. Never let someone who has not invested themselves discourage you.

Posting Your Ads

When posting your ad at the Off-Campus Housing Department, follow the guidelines that we've outlined in the previous chapter.

1. Call out unique features in the home, things like extra-large rooms, updated kitchen, walking distance to school, 5 bedrooms, clean bathrooms, super clean house, lots of parking, great deck, BBQ included, brand new appliances.

2. Include pictures in your ad whenever possible. Most landlords are lazy and won't go through the extra effort of uploading pictures. And we won't always put pictures of the front of the house b/c they're pretty generic, and most students don't care what the house looks like on the outside … they are more concerned with clean kitchens and washrooms, so our picture on the online ads may be something like this:

3. We use words and phrases like these to really have our ads stand out (everything must be true of course!): "stunning student rental," "perfect move-in condition," "brand new paint job," "brand new bathrooms").

Once you've figured out your strategy with the Off-Campus Housing Department then you can move to your next resource:

#2 Resource: Complimentary Online and Offline Advertising Resources

You'll be surprised at how often the Off-Campus Housing Advertising alone will generate enough leads for you (at an inexpensive price!), but you should be ready to ramp up your advertising if necessary.

And the best place to find these complimentary advertising resources will be back at Off-Campus Housing.

Right below UBC Housing's bulletin locations are additional resources where they direct students.
How convenient is that?

Everything you need is right at your fingertips.

And we've found that almost every Off-Campus Housing website will have a "Resources" or "Quicklinks" section on their site with similar lists of additional useful advertising websites.

Here's a tip for you...

We've found that over the last couple of years, www.Kijiji.ca has been one of the very best online classified ad resources for multiple property types.

And the best part, it's free.

So, we would recommend:

1. Spend some money to post your Off-Campus Housing Ad, both on its online site and on its physical posting board (if both are available).

2. Supplement with an ad on Kijiji.ca.

3. Monitor the number of calls you get and if you need to generate more. Only then spend money on some of the other resources you find.

It's always better to be ready with your research and advertising plan in advance so that you can act quickly.

Time is money after all, especially when you're dealing with vacant properties.

#3 Resource: Sign on the Lawn

Nothing beats the quality of calls you'll generate from a yard sign.

It likely won't generate more calls than other forms of advertising, but there's nothing better than a person standing in front of your property calling the number.

We've found these types of student calls to be of very high quality.

For student rental signs, we don't use anything fancy. A simple pole in the ground with a bright sign that says "For Rent" has worked magically for us.

We find many landlords get cheap and put small "For Rent" signs the size of an 8.5" x 11" sheet of paper in the window of their property.

And you can barely make out the phone number that they have on it when you're parked in front of the house.

Remember, if it's difficult to see your sign, you'll definitely get fewer calls. Make sure you have a sign that gets noticed!

A word of advice:

It seems many investors will spend a lot of money to acquire a property and then get very cheap when it comes to advertising it. Don't' let that be you!

The pole should cost you anywhere from $50 to $100 and the sign is about $10 from Home Depot.

Well worth the investment.

We always view advertising as an "investment" in our property – never as an "expense."

A few hundred dollars in advertising may generate 3 years of leases worth a total of $90,000 gross revenue for you.

Don't get stingy on your advertising. Be smart, be frugal, but don't be cheap about it.

Do you take calls live or direct them to voicemail?

We almost always direct calls to voicemail.

Part of the reason for this is that we believe "living life on our terms." And that means not being tied to a cell phone 24/7.

However, because our student rentals often have very brief advertising windows and we want to maximize our effectiveness during those times, we occasionally take calls directly to our cell phones or to someone managing the calls live for us.

For example, in some universities, the students have a habit of looking for off-campus housing at a very specific time of year.

At McMaster University in Hamilton, we found that during the first two weeks of January groups of students get together and try to find a house for themselves for the upcoming school year.

Aside: Ask Off-Campus Housing if your university or college has a time of year where groups of students are actively looking for housing. This will be your most important advertising time. This is a big, big tip for you.

So, if our current students are not returning for the next school year, we have all our advertising in place during this time and take calls live.

We realize that signing up a group of students into a house means that we can fill 6 or 7 students in one shot. And if they stay for 3 years, it can be very financially rewarding.

However, York University in Toronto doesn't have such a condensed period of time where many groups of students are looking for housing.

What that means is that students are coming and going at different schedules and your property will likely have single vacant rooms on a more frequent basis.

In those types of cases, we often use a voicemail number on our advertising and on our lawn sign because we don't want to be taking calls at all times of the day.

We then return calls once a day until our rooms are filled. You end up playing a bit more phone tag but it sure beats taking calls at all hours.

Step 2: Getting Students to Sign on the Dotted Line...

Now that you've set up your advertising and you've started taking calls, it's time to get students to your property.

Here's the single biggest tip we can give you:

Direct all students to see your property on the same day and at the same time.

When we used to show our properties to individual students, we wasted hours of our time.

Here's why:

1. If they called us looking for a full house for a group of friends, they would often have a few of the friends "scout" homes and then report back. This meant that we would have to go out of our way several times a week to show the property only to hear, "Thanks, we'll go back and discuss it with our friends and let you know." Ah!! Do you know how disheartening it can be driving home for the 10th time with no signed leases in hand!

2. Or, they would comment on some small aspect of the house. like a slightly small closet in one bedroom or a kitchen that they felt needed a small paint touch-up. And these small little items seemed to prevent them from making a decision.

3. And if we were showing a single room to someone there was no urgency for them to sign a lease with us. They likely had 10 other rooms to look at in the neighbourhood and would decide after seeing them all.

So, we decided to turn the tables in our favour and began setting all appointments on the same day and at the same time.

This removed all the little objections that students had – that were often really silly anyway.

And of course, we would address any serious issues with the property if they had a legitimate concern that was valid (a smoke alarm not working for example).

Here's how this plays out:

1. We get phone calls coming in and we let the person calling know that we'll be showing the property on Saturday at 1:00 p.m. Don't make Saturday

appointments too early for students – trust us!

2. We let them know some other people may be there.

3. If we're doing this at a time of year when a lot of groups of students are looking for properties, we may have has many as 80 students show up.

4. Or, if we're doing this for a single individual room we may only have 2 or 3 people show up.

5. We then show the property to one party or one group at a time and have everyone else wait outside.

6. This way everyone sees the demand for the property and all the little objections that they may have had are washed away.

7. We've done this several times and have been able to sign leases within 60 minutes of the first showing!

8. We then direct all other students to other properties we have in the area!

Works like a charm!

On one property, we had the same group of students in it for 2 years. When they were in their last year, we ran advertising for a new group of students.

And we went through the steps as outlined above and had new leases signed within 45 minutes of arriving at the property.

Those students then stayed for 3 years!

How's that for leveraging your time?

A possible exception to this:

If we're trying to fill a single room, it can sometimes be harder to have multiple people show up at the same time at a property. If we're unable to get a single, one-off room filled after a couple of attempts at using this strategy, we will make individual appointments until the room is filled.

However, when filling a home that has multiple rooms vacant, the above strategy cannot be beaten! We use it regularly with massive success.

We've now even started putting "open house" signs around the area the day we're doing the showing to further drive up the demand at the property.

And there you have it.

You now know more about student rental investing than a huge percentage of the population and even more than many experienced investors.

Stay tuned, because we're moving onto Lease Options in Part 4 and you won't want to miss the great gems of information we have in store for you!

Part 4:

Lease Options

Chapter 17

Lease Option Investing

In this chapter, we're going to give a 10,000-foot view of what a lease option investment strategy really is. First, you should know that it can be called many things, "lease options," "rent-to-own," "lease with the option to buy," etc. All these terms are referring to the same type of investment.

The reason that we personally use the term "rent-to-own" is really for marketing. When you're advertising for tenants to move into the home (we call them tenant buyers), it's much easier to have them understand the concept when you say "rent-to-own."

Plus, here's a super important reason and a BIG tip for you.

Using "Rent to Own" in your advertising of the home will get you many more calls than any other description.

And remember, the landlord with the most calls wins! Unfortunately, there was a lot of money spent on advertising for us to figure this out. But now that we know it let's use it!

Like any other investment, when you are learning something new you really want to understand the strategy to see if it fits into your portfolio or goals.

Remember, not everyone's portfolio is going to be the same, so what may fit into someone else's portfolio might not fit into yours. This strategy may not be something you are interested in and we're going to discuss some of the pros and cons as well.

Here's how this lease option – oops, sorry, rent-to-own thing works.

It is really a two-part process.

First, you are renting out the home to a tenant. Second, at the same time, you are signing a separate agreement that's giving them the option to buy the home for a predetermined price during their tenancy.

It sounds simple because it is!

You can set up the length of the lease or rent-to-own program however you would like. One, two, or three-year terms are the most common.

The opportunity to sign up tenants for longer contracts than the standard one-year term in most regular rental programs is one of the obvious benefits of using rent-to-own programs.

Instead of thinking about a lease renewal every year it may not even cross your mind for THREE!

Back to the two-part process.

The first is no different than the standard procedure of renting out your home to a tenant. There is a lease agreement to sign and most of the time it won't be any different than the one you have used for any other rental property.

But don't forget to change the address… it may sound silly, but it has happened before!

In the second part, you are completing an "Option to Purchase" agreement. This is where your tenant agrees to a potential purchase of your home in the future.

Typically, there is a payment from them for the privilege of having this option to purchase in place.

The money the tenant pays is applied to the down payment the tenant would use when they purchase the property.

For example, let's pretend a tenant gives you $6,500 for the option to purchase a home in the future for $450,000. And that tenant plans to purchase the home with a 5% down payment ($22,500).

When it came time to purchase the home, they would only need another $16,000 because they already gave you the rest of the money before moving in.

It is very similar to taking profit up front, which is a great thing!

But we are giving up something in exchange for this payment. Remember it has to be win/win for it to work.

We are giving up some of our control over the property.

We always keep the title of the property in our name but now we have a signed agreement in place that gives the tenant the legal right to purchase the property for the duration of the option to purchase agreement we signed.

Normally this isn't an issue because we plan on owning the property for the whole time and reaping the rewards of the sale.

However, if we were looking to sell the property, we would have to disclose the fact that there is an option to purchase agreement in place. This agreement gives the tenant the legal right to be able to purchase the property for the price you set in the agreement, with any conditions that you have agreed to as well.

This option to purchase agreement hanging over the property may not be appealing to a potential buyer so the property may not be as attractive should you wish to sell it.

A good question is, "why would we do something like this?" We have already determined that having control over your investments is a good thing.

It is similar to putting your rental property on a strength and conditioning program. Or in some sports, they take it to the next level, which is why we often look at these types of investments as a 'rental property on steroids.'

Using rent-to-own programs will increase your cash flow on the property by having tenants give you a down payment for the option to buy the home. So, you are bulking up your profit.

Now for an important point.

This down payment money is non-refundable.

Yes, circumstances can change in two or three years and the tenant may not end up purchasing your property. But they have paid for you to give up control of the property.

We are very upfront about this with potential tenants, so they are aware of the details. Many view it as an opportunity to 'test drive' the home with the major repairs still being our responsibility as the homeowner.

If your tenant decides not to purchase, the money they paid you for the option becomes 100% profit.

As an investor, this can be very appealing because the money acts as a built-in insurance policy on the home. If the tenant decides to move to another city, any advertising or carrying costs incurred to find another tenant should be covered by the initial down payment you received before the initial tenant moved in.

This process is very similar to purchasing a stock option. A stock option is an investment where you can buy the option to purchase stock in the future at a specific price that you set out today.

We are using the same principle and applying it to real estate.

But that's not the only way we are able to **bulk up** our profits using a rent-to-own strategy.

We usually offer the home for rent at a higher price than the average in the area, which will increase our cash flow. To do this we offer monthly credits to the tenant that will be applied to the future down payment on the property.

Every time the tenant pays their rent on time, we offer them a specific amount of money towards the down payment. This helps create a win/win scenario.

The tenant is able to have money go towards the purchase of the home, and the investor is able to generate more profit every month.

As with anything else, this approach has both pros and cons. Let's take a look at them:

Rent-to-Own 'Pros'

1) **Financial** – Since we have covered this already we won't dwell on it anymore.

2) **Property Maintenance** – Generally, a tenant will take better care of the home because they view it as their own. We explain up front that we view this as their house so if little things come up they are responsible for them (usually a $200 limit). But if any major repairs arise, we are still the formal owners and it is our responsibility. We have seen tenants finish basements, pave driveways, replace fences, etc. (But we know the major repairs will be limited since we invested in a solid home from the beginning.)

   Often a rent-to-own program allows for a bit more of a hands-off approach to property management since the tenant can be more proactive.

3) **Screening Process** – When you are asking for a few thousand dollars in addition to rent before a tenant moves in, it will usually screen out many low-end tenants.

Our experience has shown us that the worst tenants would not be willing to part with any extra cash other than rent.

There are extreme examples in all cases. We have seen rent-to-own tenants spend thousands on home upgrades and we've come across a few that make a mess. But the average rent-to-own tenant has been a higher quality in most cases we have come across.

4) **Commitment** – The tenants are more committed to the home because they are both financially and emotionally involved in, it.

On top of being more financially invested in this property because of the down payment, they now have the pride of having their own home. Often it will be the first time that they've ever been able to purchase a home (or been so close to purchasing a home with your help and the rent-to-own strategy).

This makes them emotionally committed as well. There have been times when tenants have had tears in their eyes when we have handed over the keys because they're so happy to have a place of their own. They are proud that they can have family over for a Christmas dinner or other holidays.

Rent-to-Own "Cons"

1) **Control** – As we spoke about earlier, we are giving up some flexibility with the property.

2) **Still Work Involved** – This really isn't a negative but more a point to remember.

There still are some typical landlord risks. If the furnace breaks down, you're responsible for it. If a tornado comes along and rips off a roof (unlikely), you're responsible for it. Yes, these are pretty extreme examples, but those types of typical landlord responsibilities don't go away. Usually, they're reduced because the tenant is more committed to the home.

3) **Long-Term Sacrifice?** - As we have discussed many times, real wealth in real estate comes from acquiring properties that pay for themselves and make you monthly cash flow over time.

   With a rent-to-own scenario that is the case, but only for short periods of time because the tenant has the potential to buy the home after only a couple of years. So, you may not be able to acquire as much equity as you would like before it sells.

   The key point to remember is that this isn't really a short-term investment, but it's not a long-term investment either. It's somewhere in the middle.

There is a lot of flexibility using the rent-to-own approach that can be applied to other investments as well. In fact, some of our members have taken this approach and applied it to underperforming rental properties.

They have been able to increase cash flow and get out of a rental situation that they were not happy about because they now have a better understanding of real estate investing. They better understand how the numbers work and realize that a different property can be making much more cash flow for them, so they are trying to cash out of their current investment through a rent-to-own strategy and move on to new investments.

That's our 10,000-foot view of lease option investing or the rent-to-own approach. As we dive in for a closer look, we will cover all the details. Things like the types of people who look for rent-to-own homes, the documents involved, marketing strategies, and specialized negotiation tactics.

Chapter 18

Lease Option Fundamentals

"Who are the right candidates for Lease / Option properties anyway?"

Your ideal tenant for a lease/option (rent-to-own) can be summarized with this: Good Income but Bad Credit.

That's what you're looking for.

Someone who is making enough money to support the monthly rental amount but for some reason has bad credit.

And their bad credit is preventing them from:

1. Getting a mortgage or,
2. Getting a reasonable interest rate on a mortgage.

A while back, one of our tenants in a lease/option property was an accountant. He had very good income, took trips to Las Vegas and down south, bought new cars, and appliances, but he had poor credit.

A divorce situation had left him with the desire to get a home for his children in a specific area of town so they could stay in the same schools – but the interest rate on the mortgage he could qualify for was about 5% higher than "normal."

What do we mean by "bad credit?"

In Canada, a credit score is a numerical expression of your credit files that is intended to report your "creditworthiness."

Canadian lenders use these scores, sometimes called FICO scores because of the system used to create them, to evaluate the potential risk of lending money to you.

Your score plays a large role in determining if you qualify for a mortgage or loan, with what interest rate, and for what amount.

The system used in Canada is fairly similar to the one used in the United States with the same major reporting agencies: Equifax and Transunion.

And in Canada, you are allowed to pull your credit yourself as many times as you'd like for free as long as that request is made to either Equifax or Transunion in writing.

A perfect score is 900.
And the lowest possible score that we're aware of is 300.

Most banks treat anyone with over a score of 680 or higher as "good credit" and most, if not all, of the best mortgage and loan products, are available to people with "good credit."

If your score is between 650 and 680, you still have decent credit, but some mortgage products may not be available to you.

And if your score is below 650, you can still get a mortgage, but you won't qualify for many of the mortgages available from banks and brokers.

The Canadian Government offers a free publication called "Understanding Your Credit Report and Credit Score" which is very useful.

You can find this and more great information by visiting: www.Canada.ca/en/services/finance/debt.html

The main reasons behind a person having a low credit score are:

1. Personal bankruptcy

2. Business bankruptcy that has affected them personally because loans were personally guaranteed

3. Divorce

4. Non-disclosure of income to the Canadian Revenue Agency (We've seen this many times with seasonal workers in trades like roofing and outdoor construction.)

Most landlords are turned off by the word "bankruptcy" in any tenant's profile, but by simply asking for some information about their background you'll get an idea if the reasons behind their bankruptcy were a "one-time occurrence" or a "pattern of behaviour."

If someone has declared bankruptcy several times, it's likely that they'll do it again.

However, if a possible tenant was running a business that had a bad spell, that doesn't mean they are destined to repeat it.

Use your judgment.

Many good people have had an event in their lives that left them with low credit scores.

Let's profile your <u>ideal tenant</u> for a Lease / Option property:

1. They are stable in their lives and in their jobs.

2. They have the financial ability to pay monthly rent.

3. They will appreciate and care for the home (the best sign for this is by examining their level of their excitement for the property).

4. Many times, but not always, the best tenants for Lease/Options are 1st time home buyers.

5. They have a desire to own a home but can't get lending from a bank.

6. They can't raise money for a down payment because of recent personal or business events (but have the ability to save).

7. They are looking to improve their situation in life.

It's somewhat difficult to make a "cookie cutter" template for the perfect tenant in a Lease/Option.

The points listed above create a "gut feeling" for the type of person the tenant is and we use that as 50% of our decision-making process.

The other 50% is dictated by the facts.

And those are:

- What is their income level?
- How long have they been generating that amount of income?

We want to "think like the bank" in these situations.

Here in Ontario tenants often use 50% of their income for housing. Although that's fine and dandy, we still want to use a more conservative percentage when looking at how much of their monthly income will be used for rent.

So, if we can see that a tenant would be using only 30% - 33% of their income towards the monthly rent, we feel good about their ability to pay on a regular basis.

The ratio of 30% - 33% is the same one used by many financial institutions when qualifying people for a mortgage.

Often, our lease/option homes are so nice and so well located that we'll have tenants, who clearly cannot afford the property, fill out applications.

We feel it's our duty to inform them of our concerns with their ability to pay rent.

We would much rather have this talk up front with a tenant then have someone who can't afford the rent move in only to have them move out three months later.

Got that all?

You're looking for good income and poor credit.

Many good people are walking around in these situations and it's a pleasure to be able to help them.

What Type of Properties Fit This Model the Best?

Now that we know more about the type of person looking to for a Lease/Option property, let's cover which properties work best.

There are two important angles to this.

1. You want to protect your own investment by investing in real estate that always has the highest demand. And that's the starter home category.

2. And second, you want a property that appeals to your prospective tenants – to your "market."

Often, people will buy a property because it's a "good deal." But as we've discussed in previous chapters, most "good deals" are that way for a reason. There's likely something about the property that needs improving.

We are <u>very careful</u> to buy good properties when using Lease/Option strategies because if the tenant does not buy the property at the end of the lease, we want to be able to "re-rent" the property easily.

Although we expect cosmetic improvements will be necessary (carpet cleaning, new paint, etc.), we want "the bones" of the house to be excellent.

So, things like foundation, roof, street location, curb appeal, windows, furnace, plumbing, and electrical should all have a lifespan of longer than the lease period.

If we're leasing out a property on a three-year lease, we prefer that 80% of the above items have a lifespan of double our lease.

We know that it's impossible to find a "perfect property" and if the foundation, furnace, plumbing and electrical are in good shape perhaps we'll accept a roof with only four years of life on it.

Otherwise, we'll spend years looking for the perfect property.

What are some of the characteristics of a good Lease/Option property?

Here's what we've found:

1. They are in a great neighbourhood.
2. They have a good looking cosmetic interior.
3. Nice curb appeal.
4. No specific style (side-split, back-split, townhome, bungalow etc.).
5. Minimum of 3 bedrooms.
6. Ideally 2 bathrooms.
7. Parking.

Remember earlier how we mentioned that you're looking for a home in the "starter home" category?

Well, here's a tip…

Focus on the upper-end of that category.

Most investors focus on low-end, cheap starter homes.

Instead, we'll look at an area, decide what the starter home is and then move to the upper end of that "class" of home.

Instead of choosing the cheapest townhomes possible we'll find the newer more updated townhomes.

These tend to be in nice areas, which attract tenants.

And they rent out faster because they're in such good condition.

Here's a picture of an actual lease/option property in Burlington, Ontario (a suburb on the west side of Toronto):

It's a newer property, so all the important pieces are in good shape (foundation, roof, plumbing, electrical).

The street appeal is good, and it's in a good area with good schools.

Further west in Burlington, we can find older, cheaper townhomes, but they won't attract the "good income" tenants that we're looking for.

Remember, tenants in lease/option properties are paying higher than average rent. In return, they want to live in a good area.

And when you're investing in the upper end of the starter home market, you'll avoid competition with many other rental properties because most other investors are buying the cheapest properties around.

Now, if we're in an area where townhomes aren't "the norm" and there are more detached houses in the community, we'll buy a slightly larger starter home in a slightly better area.

Our acquisition costs will be higher, but long-term we'll have a stronger real estate portfolio.

Here's an example of such a home in Brantford, Ontario:

This is a 4-level side-split on a huge corner lot. There are smaller, cheaper homes about 15-minutes away, but we know that homes on the north side of the highway in this community demand better resale and rent prices.

So that's where we want to be.

A larger home like this also gives the tenants options to have older kids and in-laws live with them. This is not only nice for the family but increases the amount of family income.

Here's another lease/option property.

This is in Waterdown, Ontario and was picked out by the tenants themselves, and approved by the investor.

They gave the investor a large option fee and paid for first and last month's rent before the investor even took possession of the property.

We'll describe the details of how this was accomplished in a future lesson.

And here's another property in Hamilton, Ontario in an area known as the "Hamilton Mountain."

This property was purchased "on the mountain" instead of the downtown area because it's generally a nicer area with higher appreciation.

Many investors purchase lower-priced single-family homes in this community closer to the downtown core, but that area doesn't match the "good area, good homes" criteria that we know work so well with Lease/Options.

And although this is a slightly larger home (it's a semi-detached 4-level back-split), it is still in the starter home category that we're looking for.

Chapter 19

How to Rent Your Home Fast & for Top Dollar

In the last chapter, we focused on finding your "ideal tenant" and "selecting the proper property."

We're going to thread continuing discussions of those two points over the next couple of chapters.

In this chapter, we begin a critical portion of our Lease/Option discussions…

How to Fill Your Home Fast & For Top Dollar

We're going to break this down into bite-sized steps together. Here's a quick summary of what we're going to cover:

1. Yard Signs & Types of Phone Numbers

2. Newspaper Classified Ads & Voice Mail Boxes

3. Online Classified Ads

4. Calling Tenant Leads Back – Most Common Mistakes!

5. Sign-In Forms and Why We Use Them

6. Creating the Proper Environment in The House

7. Lease/Option Program Description using Flyers

8. The Application

9. Checking Credit

10. Taking Deposits to Hold a Property

There are a lot of juicy goodies to cover, so let's get busy.

Yard Signs & Types of Phone Numbers

Once you have found your property and have taken possession of it, you need to get the word out about what you are doing as soon as possible.

A good yard sign is still one of the very best ways to attract quality tenants.

And for some reason, investors often overlook it.

Before we actually show you a few examples, let us share a couple of stories with you about the importance of yard signs.

A few years ago, we were working with a couple of investors who were having trouble filling their property.

They had been advertising for several weeks and were getting people out to the property but just couldn't get a tenant that was interested in their Lease/Option home.

(We began working with them and quickly noticed that the environment that they were creating inside the property was a major problem – and we'll discuss this in detail a little later.)

And they didn't have a yard sign on the front lawn.

They hadn't "gotten around to it."

When you are trying to fill a property, whether it's a single-family home, triplex, a student rental, or an apartment building, you MUST get the word out about your property to the immediate local neighbourhood.

Why?

Because it's been proven to us time and time again that <u>the people closest to your property</u> end up being your <u>best source of leads</u>.

Either they will be interested in the property themselves or they'll have a friend who is.

After we finally convinced these two investors to put up a yard sign, they ended up getting a lease agreement, and an option agreement signed the next week.

One more for you…

The very same investors realized how important a yard sign was on another vacancy that they had a few months later (on a different property):

Learning from their lesson they quickly put up a yard sign letting everyone in the area know that the property was available and <u>the next-door neighbour</u> ended up calling his brother and getting him to "rent-to-own" the property using a Lease/Option!

Needless to say, we believe yard signs are a mandatory component of renting out all properties.

Side Note: Here's a little tip. Don't stop at yard signs. We've also had success with small directional arrows with the words "Rent to Own" on them spread around the neighbourhood. This works especially well if your property is on a quiet street and doesn't get much traffic. These signs may get taken down by neighbours, so always ask for permission if putting it on someone else's lawn. And the city may also remove them – so be aware that you'll likely lose a few after a few days. But the payoff is worth it.

24-Hour Message

There's a couple of key points about these signs that should be discussed.

1. Earlier, we mentioned that on all signs we put "Rent to Own" instead of "Lease/Option." Very few people understand what a lease/option is so we use more common language.

2. "All Credit Scores Welcome," or "No Banks Needed," or "Bad Credit OK" on the sign is our way of communicating that you don't have to have perfect credit to qualify for our home.

3. And lastly, but most importantly, we have found that when we include the words "24 Hour Message" on our sign we get more calls.

There's something about knowing that you won't have to talk to a live person when you call that drives a higher call volume.

And your goal is to get as many calls as humanly possible.

You are in competition against all other available properties, so you want to use every slight edge that you can to drive up the number of people that call the number on your sign.

Let's take a look at some signs…

At the top of this picture, you'll notice a type of "directional sign" that was used to drive traffic to the property.

At the bottom of this picture, you'll see another layout for a yard sign. This one is totally different, but still has the key ingredients:

1. The words "Rent to Own"
2. 24-Hour Message is clearly displayed
3. All Credit Welcome is mentioned on the sign.

You'll also notice that on these signs a Toll-Free number is being used.

We've noticed NO difference in response to signs using Toll-Free numbers.

We have even used numbers that are long distance and still had a strong amount of calls off of our advertising.

One last note about signs…

Make sure you invest in a good strong sign with a metal stand. The sign and the stand together should cost you anywhere from $80 to $130 but no more.

We have seen many investors buy small wire stands with plastic "bag signs" draped over the wire. These signs blow over. They are good enough to use for directional signs but don't use cheap signs as your main yard sign.

A sign that is lying on the ground is of no use to you. Spend the money on a professional yard sign.

Newspaper Classified Ads

The next thing to consider is advertising in the local newspapers.

We covered this type of advertising in Chapter 4, but here's an example of an ad for a rent-to-own property...

Some notes:

1. Notice that the words "Rent to Own" are really standing out. We initially tried using the words "Lease Option" or "For Rent with an Option to Buy" and our call volume wasn't as good. The words "Rent to Own" are the best.

2. Also, you'll see that we put "24 Message" or "24hr MSG" in the ads – this drives up response to our advertising.

3. In classified advertising, we usually go with the more direct "Bad Credit OK" instead of the politer version we use on Yard Signs of "All Credit Accepted."

4. We have tested these types of ads in the "Houses for Sale" section and the "Houses for Rent" section and the "Houses for Rent" section always gets more calls.

5. Some papers charge too much for borders and shading, so instead, we go with the standard graphics that they offer. These graphics usually are large words above your little ad that say: "Amazing" or "LOOK." We'll do whatever we need to get our ads to stand out from the others.

Remember: Advertising is an <u>investment</u> and not an <u>expense</u>.

Chapter 20

Mastering Online Exposure & Call Backs

Let's jump right in where we left off...

Online Classified Ads

We treat online ads very similar to offline ads. They must contain the same ingredients:

a. Use the words "Rent to Own" to describe what you're offering.

b. Highlight any unique characteristics of your property (e.g. Large backyard, big deck for BBQs, extra bedroom, large driveway, renovated kitchen/bathroom/basement, new paint etc.)

c. We tend to use the words "move-in condition" in our ads regularly to highlight the fact that the property is not a run-down rental property.

d. Always include the words "24-hour message" if you're using a voicemail box to capture your leads.

e. And we'll mention that "Bad Credit is OK" to highlight.

The best websites in Canada for advertising Lease/Option Properties are:

1. Kijiji.ca (FREE)

This site has by far the most traffic and activity for rentals in Canada right now.

2. GottaRent.com (approx. $30/month)

Gottarent.com has a lot of apartments listed but works for renting out single-family homes as well.

3. YourClassifieds.ca (one website for multiple communities – varying prices)

A quick Google search for "local classified" ads will turn up multiple sources of online classified services like this one.

4. Craigslist.ca (FREE)

Craigslist has been in the "free online ads" world for a long time. However, our tests show that the responses you get from Craigslist.ca will be low.

Kijiji.ca is constantly improving its website, and now you can include more than two pictures.

Here's a tip when sharing pictures online…

Don't use all your best pictures on the ad right away. Especially when using FREE classified ad websites like Kijiji.ca.

Why?

Because on free online ad websites your ad will quickly disappear onto page 2 and then page 3 and so on.

The principles covered in Chapter 4 for online advertising are the same for rent-to-own properties.

Your Voice Mail Script for Lease/Option Advertisements

If you're going to use a voicemail box to capture incoming leads, here's a sample voicemail script that you can use:

Thank you for calling about our beautiful Rent-to-Own Home.

We have designed a special Rent-to-Own Program that will help you get into this home today!

Our program is a two or three-year program that provides you time to work through any current credit report issues that you might have.

During the two or three-year program, we will work hand and hand with a lender specializing in helping buyers qualify for their own homes.

The home that is currently available for this special Rent-to-Own program is located _____ *<mention the major intersection only, not the full address. You want as many people leaving messages as possible so you can speak to them personally>*

This lovely home offers: _____ *<along with a standard description of how many bedrooms mention emotional things, patio, walkways, upgraded kitchen, bathrooms, large trees, fenced yard, shopping close by, transit close by>*

To schedule a time to walk through and view this lovely home, please leave your **name and both a day & evening phone number** at the tone.

In addition, please leave in your message the amount of money that you have available to put down on this home. Please understand that the larger down payment you can raise to put towards this home, the more likely it is that we will select you for this home.

Thanks for calling and we look forward to helping you!

There are a few critical points to talk about here...

First, notice that we don't mention the full address? Why do we do that?

Because if you hand out the address in the voicemail message, we found that we get lots of hang-ups.

People will take the address and drive by the property before they decide to leave a message.

And the chance of them losing the little sticky note that they write the address on is high.

So, we don't give the address, just a major intersection. That way they're more inclined to leave a message to speak with us.

When we call back we're very friendly and personable. We then share the address and set an appointment. It's during our return phone call that we develop a rapport with people.

Second, in the second last paragraph, we ask for money

down. This money is to be used as the "option fee" (which we will cover in detail shortly!).

We found that when we didn't have this paragraph in our voicemail messages people would be surprised when we asked them to put down an option fee.

This simple addition really made people much more receptive to the process.

Calling Possible Tenants for Lease/Option Properties

This is the most important step.

Call all leads back within 24-hours whenever possible. Any longer and people either move on or are more difficult to get a hold of.

Ensure you are being casual and friendly when you call back. You want to develop rapport and build relationships with people that you call.

People will be more open to trusting you if you are very straightforward and friendly.

We've broken down each situation for you…

<u>Situation #1</u>: You get someone on the phone live!

Hi, can I speak with _____?

Oh, hi, my name is _____ and I'm returning your call about the rent-to-own home on/near
_____.

I'm just calling back to answer any questions and be as helpful as possible.

Here are the most common questions you will receive...

Question: How many bedrooms, what type of home is it?

Answer: Describe the home as best as you can and make sure you highlight any unique things (e.g. the basement is finished, fresh paint, bathroom(s) are updated, huge backyard, great patio, close to transportation, close to shops, good street, bigger than normal, bright, clean, move in condition etc.).

Question: How does this rent-to-own thing work?

Answer: I haven't set up the final numbers yet but basically you pay a monthly rent and a portion of that goes towards to the purchase price. There will be 2 or 3 different rental amounts to choose from. I'm going to be at the property on _____ at _____am/pm, why don't you just stop on by? Who knows... you may not even like the place! But I can tell you that it's a really beautiful home.

Question: Why do you need a deposit or down payment?

Answer: The only reason we ask for a down payment is to ensure you're serious about the home. That money makes up the option fee that allows you to buy the home. I'm busy and don't want to be back here after 3 months if you move out. I just want to know that this is the right home for you and you're serious about buying it at the end of the rent. That's basically it. By the way, I've found that whenever we get a down payment, whoever moves in seems to really take care of the place very well. It seems to work for both of us. And the down payment goes towards the purchase at the end, so it's credited back to you.

Answer Questions & Guide to an appointment

Do you think you can make it out on _____ at
_____am/pm?

(If yes…) OK, good. Can I ask a favour? Here's my cell
phone number. If you can't make it for whatever reason,
can you please call me? Because it will save me some
time.

(If no…) OK, well I'll be back out there on _____ at
_____ am/pm? Does that work better?

Important Notes:

1. We make a conscious effort to focus on setting
    appointments for the home. We used to explain every
    single detail of Lease/Options over the phone and just
    confused people. We now go through all details of the
    agreements when we're signing them. We've learned
    that it's much more effective to take one baby step at a
    time and not try and accomplish too much when
    returning phone calls. Your strategy around this will
    depend on your own style – but that's what works well
    for us.

2. We always try and set multiple appointments at the
    same time. This creates an environment where people
    are more likely to make decisions, and it saves us
    countless trips back and forth to the property. This is
    one of the biggest tips that we can offer you.

3. We typically will not leave voicemails when we return calls unless we've tried to get a hold of the person two times previously. On the third call, we'll leave the address, directions and the day/time that we'll be there. We have filled multiple properties from people coming out to a property because of a voice mail message they received from us.

Situation #2: You get voicemail

Always try and call back at least twice. It's much better if you speak to someone live.

So, don't leave a voicemail on your first or second attempt.

If on the third try you get voicemail, here's a sample message:

"Hi, I'm returning your call about the rent-to-own ad. My name is _____ and I'm going to be at the property on _____ at _____ am/pm. I will be there for a short amount of time but feel free to stop by and check out the place. I can give you a little sheet explaining how the rent-to-own program works at that time as well. The house is located at _____, it's near _____, the best way to get there is _____.
Call me for directions if you need more detail, my cell phone is _____."

Situation #3: Email Responses to Leads from any Classified Ads

Typical Questions via email:

- Where is the home?
- How much is it?
- How many bedrooms?

Although the questions will be brief don't discount these leads. Many tenants are coming from web leads.

You want your email to give some information but basically guide them to the house.

Email Response:

The home has 3 bedrooms/It's near _____/Typical rent in the area is _____

The Rent-to-Own program is pretty simple. Each month a portion of your rent goes towards the purchase of the home.

I'm going to be out there on _____ at ____am/pm sharp.

You can come on by and check it out. I'll have all the information on a little sheet there that I can hand you.

Let me know if you would like the address. And you can get more details by calling the information message I have set up on this 24hr message line: XXX-XXX-XXXX.

Chapter 21

Walking Possible Tenants Through Their Option

We've been working our way through this laundry list of components that create successful Lease/Option (rent-to-own) investment properties.

In this chapter, we're going to zero in on **Creating the Proper Environment in The House** and **Lease/Option Program Description using Flyers**.

We are big believers in "systems," and we don't treat this as a hobby. The nice thing about having a system outlined for your investment property is that anytime you want to execute that system, you can pull out the steps and get busy.

There's no thinking required, which is sometimes a good thing.

We all tend to over complicate matters and can easily get stressed out when we don't know where to begin.

Treat these steps as your business process for Lease/Option properties.

Creating the Proper Environment in The House

After you called possible tenants back and set appointments for them to come to your property (hopefully, all at the same time!), you want to make sure you create the right atmosphere at the home.

The day before you go to meet your appointments, ensure the house will be in good showing condition. Clean and neat. If you have followed our "buy a good house in a good area" advice, you have a great property so there is likely not much to do.

Open all windows to let in fresh air.

Turn on any fireplaces and ceiling fans.

Make sure every single light in the whole house is turned on, even if it is a bright and sunny day. Lighting enhances the look of the house – turn them on!

If it's winter, make sure the house is warm. If it's summer, try and cool the house and get a draft through it or turn on the air conditioning.

Your house will likely be one of the best on the street, so feel proud, confident and speak with conviction. It's a great one. The people you will be meeting at the property will likely be coming from a rental unit somewhere to one of the best homes on the street.

You have a good product, be proud.

The day before, call your best leads and remind them of the time you are meeting.

And remember this: When you're at the home be casual and friendly, don't come across as the *"professional"* real estate person.

Be the first to say "hi" and let them walk through the house themselves.

One of the last steps is to put out a sign-in sheet.

The sign in form is used as a critical part in the system.

It gets your leads to commit, on paper, how much they can put towards the option fee. They also see how much other people are committing.

They have heard about the option fee on your voicemail message and they are being confronted by it again on the sign-in sheet.

By the time you actually speak with them, they should be well aware that there is a down payment involved.

This makes the entire system work smoothly.

Here's what the sign-in sheet looks like...

NAME	PHONE	AMOUNT OF UPFRONT $	HOW DID YOU HEAR ABOUT PROPERTY? (check one)
			▢ Classified Ad ▢ Signs ▢ Other ___
			▢ Classified Ad ▢ Signs ▢ Other ___
			▢ Classified Ad ▢ Signs ▢ Other ___
			▢ Classified Ad ▢ Signs ▢ Other ___
			▢ Classified Ad ▢ Signs ▢ Other ___
			▢ Classified Ad ▢ Signs ▢ Other ___
			▢ Classified Ad ▢ Signs ▢ Other ___
			▢ Classified Ad ▢ Signs ▢ Other ___
			▢ Classified Ad ▢ Signs ▢ Other ___

The sign-in sheet also lets you track who comes and goes. And it allows you to track your advertising. You'll be amazed at how valuable it turns out to be.

Don't worry if possible tenants don't fill out the "amount of upfront money" column. Your goal is for them to see it. If they leave it blank, they've still seen that some amount of upfront money is required.

By seeing that on the sign-in sheet, they won't be surprised when they see it on the application.

Lease/Option Program Description using Flyers

After your appointments have signed in, allow them to do a "self-guided" tour of the property.

No one wants you to hang on their back while they are walking around. Let them check the home out and talk about it in private.

Your role at this time is to hang out in the kitchen and be ready to handle questions.

After they are done looking around, the best approach to begin a conversation is simply by asking, *"Would you like to know a bit more about how the rent-to-own program works?"*

Ninety-nine percent of the time you'll get a positive response to this.

At this point, we originally tried to verbally explain all the numbers and the buyout prices and the credits, but it just got too complicated.

So instead, we now outline everything on a little flyer (a single sheet of paper) that looks like this:

RENT-TO-OWN HOME SAVINGS PROGRAM
PROPERTY ADDRESS:

_____

Depending on which savings program you select, you can start automatically earning credits towards your down payment and ultimate purchase of this lovely home. You can move in now and as you make your monthly house payment earn hundreds of dollars towards your down payment and purchase this home. In fact, many of our Rent-to-Own Buyers use the time during the Rent-to-Own Program to earn thousands of dollars in credits and improve credit issues (or resolve any uncertainties). You can purchase this lovely home at any point during the Rent-to-Own Program. There is no obligation for you to buy the home, only an option.

If you purchase the home within the second year, your price is
_____.

If you purchase this home during your third year, your price is
_____.

	"NO" SAVINGS PROGRAM	"GOLD" SAVINGS PROGRAM	"SUPER" SAVINGS PROGRAM
Monthly House Payment:			
Monthly Savings Credit Earned:			
Two Year Savings Credit Earned:			
Three Year Savings Credit Earned:			

As you can see in the above chart, if you select the "No" Savings Program above, you will pay the lowest each month; however, you will not earn any monthly credits towards your purchase. If you select the "Gold" Savings Program you will be eligible to earn monthly credits towards your down payment. However, the best and fastest way for you to be able to purchase this home is through the "Super" Savings Program.

WHY YOU SHOULD CONSIDER A "RENT-TO-OWN PROGRAM" INSTEAD OF RENTING!!!

- **Rent Credits:** Each month a big chunk of your rent could get credited toward the possible purchase of your home, allowing you to build equity in your home faster than with a traditional mortgage – no more wasting all of your money on rent.
- **Improving Your Property:** Because you may own this property soon, any improvements you do that increase the value of the property may help you build more equity for yourself.
- **No banks:** You don't have to qualify with a lender today. You can move in without bank approval.
- **Own Your Own Home:** You enjoy the benefits of owning your home before you ever buy it!
- **Flexibility:** You have total flexibility: You have the option to buy your home, not the obligation!
- **Your Credit:** You are creating a strong credit reference while you are renting to own!

Note: If you should decide not to purchase this home during the Rent-to-Own Program, your earned credit will be considered rent and not refunded to you.

Let's go over each section of the flyer together...

Buy-Out Prices:

If you purchase this home within the second year, your price is **X**.

If you purchase this home during your third year, your price is **Y**.

In this area, we enter the prices that the tenants can purchase the home. We usually appreciate the home at 5% a year.

In this example, we are going to sign a 3-year lease with the tenant and they will have the option to buy the home at any time before the end of year 2 at price **X** and at any time during year 3 for price **Y**.

Monthly Prices & Credits...

	"NO" SAVINGS PROGRAM	"GOLD" SAVINGS PROGRAM	"SUPER" SAVINGS PROGRAM
Monthly House Payment:	$1,500	$1,650	$1,750
Monthly Savings Credit Earned:	$0	$200	$400
Two Year Savings Credit Earned:	$0	$4,800	$9,600
Three Year Savings Credit Earned:	$0	$7,200	$14,400

We've filled out some sample numbers.

In this example, we've used $1,500 for the "No" Savings program. The purpose of this column is to show what comparable homes rent for in the area.

Then, next to the Two & Three Year Credits, we enter in $0. This is to highlight the point that under a regular rental program they would not be earning any credits towards the purchase of the property.

We then explain that this home is available with one of two Rent-to-Own programs, they can choose from either the "Gold" or "Super" program.

Key Points:

- We are very careful to explain that they have the "option" to purchase the home. They are not "obligated" to purchase it.

- We also explain that an "option agreement" requires a fee. The option fee is non-refundable, so we are clear to go over that point with the tenant.

- We are looking for 2% to 5% of the value of the property as the option fee. 2% to 3% is most common.

- The option money can be used towards the down payment or can be used to reduce the buyout price. Whichever they prefer. We realize that Canadian banks change their rules, so we explain up front that we cannot guarantee that the option fee can be used towards the down payment because banks can change their rules without notice. But it can always be used to reduce the purchase price.

Determining the Monthly Rent & Credits

Our first step in determining what monthly amounts we'll ask for is to scout the area for rental properties and find out what they are renting for.

Let's say a 3-bedroom home in the area of our property is renting for $1,500 per month.

We would then add anywhere from $150 to $400 on top of that amount for our Rent-to-Own programs.

We'll test the "Gold" program at $1,650 and the "Super" at something like $1,750 and see what the response is.

Important Point: Many investors get frustrated with Lease/Options because nine out of ten tenants will come to the property and not be able to afford those monthly amounts. You have to accept that you're looking for that 5% or 10% of the rental pool that meets your criteria.

We know of investors who will add on $800 or more, but we find that's excessive and eliminates some very good income-earning tenants.

These numbers will vary by city. In Vancouver, we know of investors getting $2,900 per month for a 3-bedroom townhome in the city.

Let us share a quick story with you...

We were asking for $1,650 for a single-family home in Hamilton, Ontario. This was our "Gold" program.

A lady walked into the home and explained to us that we would never get that amount because homes in the area rent for $1,200.

We replied that although that may be true the costs to carry this home was closer to $1,400, and if they couldn't afford to pay $1,650 for the home plus utilities there was no chance they would be in a position to purchase the home.

We continued to explain that the program is really designed to get them into home ownership and the monthly rental amounts should be viewed from that perspective.

She promptly left the property, and 3 days later we rented it out for $1,650 and received a $10,000 upfront option fee.

Remember: You are looking for people with high income but bad credit. They really should have a gross income of three times the monthly rental amount. That's the way the banks look at mortgage applicants, and that's the way you should look at rent-to-own tenants.

The rent-to-own program will attract a lot of perpetual renters. You should be courteous and kind in explaining your programs but don't let people who can't afford the property throw you off course. The system works. Be prepared to filter through many possible tenants to find your perfect fit.

How to calculate monthly credits...

We offer 10% to 20% of the monthly rental amount in the form of credits. If we have to go higher to seal a deal, we will, but we'll never exceed more than 25%.

Why?

Because we have to be prepared to show the banks that the rental amount we were receiving was truly 10% to 20% higher than average so that they recognize the credits as down payment money. We have never been asked for this, but we want to be prepared for everything. And so should you!

These credits are not deducted and given back as cash to the tenant.

They are simply recorded in our bookkeeping each month and only used if the tenant buys the property. The credits can be used towards the down payment or towards reducing the purchase price that was agreed to.

If the tenant does not purchase the property, the credits are not something that have any cash value. We make sure to explain that point very clearly, and it's also outlined in the agreements.

Chapter 22

The Key Ingredients for Selecting Lease/Option Tenants

We've been putting together Lease/Options for a long time now. And we've seen a lot of different applications of the strategy.

One area that sometimes generates confusion is "the numbers." So, let's fix that and take another look at them right now.

Let's assume you purchase a property for $390,000

Purchase Price: $390,000
Down Payment: $78,000 (using a 20% investment mortgage)
Total Mortgage: $312,000

Mortgage Payment (25-year amortization at 3.5%): $1,557.72
Property Taxes & Insurance: $370
Total Monthly Carrying Costs: $1,927.72

Purchase Price at the End of 3yr Lease/Option: $451,500 (5% appreciation/year)
Monthly Cash Flow (Assuming Rented at $1,950): $22.28

Equity Increase (Principal Reduction from Mortgage Payments): $665/month
Total Monthly Return: $687.28/month

So, the monthly cash flow plus the monthly equity increase gives us $687.28 per month.

Now let's take a look at the buyout price if the option is exercised by the tenant to purchase the property...

We paid $390,000 for the property.

Let's break it down:

Buy Out Price at the end of 3 years: $451,500 (5% per year appreciation)
Plus, the Principal Paid Down Over the 3 Years: $23,824
Plus, the $22.28 Cash Flow Over the 3 Years: $802.08
Plus, the $5,000 collected as an Option Fee: $5,000
Equals: $481,126.08

Now, let's start <u>subtracting</u> the costs of this investment:

Beginning Total: $481,126.08
Minus Property Acquisition Cost: $390,000
Minus the "Credits" Earned by the Tenant: $10,800 ($300/month in this example)
Minus $5,000 in Price Reduction for the Option Fee Collected: $5,000
Equals a return to you of $75,326.08

So, at the end of this transaction, you're left with $75,326.08.

And there's one thing that is often forgotten in this example. You will also get your down payment back.

We did not deduct the price of the home by the amount of your down payment.

So, in the end, you'll actually have $153,326.08.

Your $78,000 down payment.

And $75,326.08 in profits.

The nice thing about Lease/Options are the multiple ways money is being generated.

You get some of your return right up front in the form of an Option Fee, you get monthly cash flow, the mortgage is being reduced so you get regular equity build-up, and if the property is bought out there is appreciation as well.

OK, we've reviewed the numbers again.

The Application & Checking Credit

After you've explained how the Rent-to-Own programs work, you need to transition to getting an application filled out.

Many investors simply explain how the programs work and then stay silent. This often leads to the tenant walking around the house some more and then simply leaving.

The name of the game is applications.

So, after you've explained the programs here's one way to transition to asking for an application:

"Hey, at this point, if you're interested, the next step is to fill out this one-page application. Standard stuff, we'll check

your credit but understand you'll likely have some credit issues, we're also interested in verifying you are who you say you are."

We want to make the tenant feel comfortable about their talking to us about their credit.

Although we will check their credit we've been advertising for bad credit, so we know it'll likely be that way.

If they have repeat bankruptcies or unpaid child support payments, then they don't meet our criteria.

Those are just personal preferences.

Ideally, they have one major incident that has affected their credit and now they're trying to recover from that. Repeat bankruptcies show a pattern of behaviour that may make it difficult for them to qualify for a mortgage.

And unpaid child support is purely a personal preference that we don't like getting involved with.

Credit reports can get tricky to read. If possible ask your mortgage broker to explain it to you.

The application that the tenant has signed gives you that permission but laws are always changing so this is one area that you'll want to have reviewed by your lawyer.

Remember: The name of the game is getting applications. Don't talk so much that you end up scaring people away. The more you talk the more you'll confuse people with your explanations of appreciation, buyouts, options and credits. Keep things simple. Be direct and always be 100% honest, but keep it simple! We've seen too many investors lose possible tenants by trying to teach a Lease/Option class in the kitchen.

Let's take a look at the application together...

Rent-to-Own FAST Approval Form

<u>EACH PERSON OVER 18 MUST COMPLETE</u>
<u>A SEPARATE APPROVAL FORM</u>

<u>PLEASE PRINT</u> - ALL information must be completed.

Full Name _____
E-Mail address: _____

Home Phone (_____) _____
Work Phone (_____) _____
Cell Phone (____) _____

Social Insurance Number _____-_____-_____
Driver's License #_____ Province: _____
Present Address

_____

City _____ Province: _____ Postal Code: _____

How Long? _____ If renting, Apartment name/location
_____ Current Payment: $ _____

Landlord/mgr.'s name _____ Phone: (__) _____

Employer: _____ Position: _____
How Long? _____

Address _____ Phone: (__) _____

Name and relationship of everyone living with you:

_____

Any pets? Describe: _____

Gross Monthly Income before deductions (include all income sources): $_____

Address you are applying for?

_____

When would you like to move in? _____

How much of a down payment can you raise? _____

Which savings program do you prefer (See Rent-to-Own Flyer)? (Circle one) 'GOLD' 'SUPER'

Is your credit, good, fair, or ugly? _____

I declare that the application is complete, true and correct and I herewith give my permission for anyone contacted (including TransUnion or Equifax) to release the credit or personal information of the undersigned applicant to Management or their authorized agents, at any time, for the purposes of entering into and continuing to offer or collect on any agreement and/or credit extended. I further authorize Management or their Authorized Agents to verify the application information including but not limited to obtaining criminal records, contacting creditors, present or former landlords, employers and personal references, whether listed or not, at the time of the application and at any time in the future, with regard to any agreement entered into with Management. Any false information will constitute grounds for rejection of this application, or Management may at any time immediately terminate any agreement entered into in reliance upon misinformation given on the application. By providing the home phone numbers and email addresses above, I/we hereby authorize the Vendor to contact me/us at my/our home phone numbers or email addresses.

Applicant's Name (Print): _____
Signature & Date: _____

NOTICE: This Rent-to-Own Home will be sold ON A FIRST COME, FIRST SERVE BASIS. If you delay in submitting this FAST Approval Form, YOU MAY LOSE THIS HOME!

Remember: The key information on this application is the information in the middle.

What is their move in date?

What is their gross family income? We're looking for at least 3 times the rental amount. So, if they choose the Gold program and it's $1,600 we're looking for a gross family income of at least $4,800.

What program are they choosing?

How much do they have as a down payment that can be used for the option fee?

If someone has $10,000 as an option fee but can't move in for 60 days, the person with $6,000 that can move in 2 weeks may be your better choice because you have less carrying costs. Don't get distracted by the biggest number. Look at all the data.

You can check credit from a number of different services, including www.RentCheckCorp.com.

Good credit is anything over a score of 680. You'll likely see scores in the low 600's, 500's and even 400's. We've even seen scores in the 300's.

Remember, you'll want someone with current experience to help you read these. We're not interested in perfect credit but if the score is extremely low it may be showing some serious issues and patterns of behaviour that will raise red flags for you.

Your mortgage broker is likely the best person to help you read these.

After you've collected applications the next step is to choose the tenant who meets your criteria the best.

Tip: Do not wait too long to follow-up. Follow-up with everyone the next day if possible. The longer you wait the more time the person you wanted to proceed with has to find another property.

And don't waste multiple days checking credit.

We always like to get some sort of deposit from the tenant if possible even **before** we check credit.

We will then return the deposit if we don't like what we see on their report.

In the past, we would lose great candidates because we took a couple of days to check credit and follow-up with them. They had already found another property. Time is of the essence during this step. Don't dilly-dally!

Also, if you're able to collect a deposit on the property of $1,000, you know you're likely dealing with a serious candidate and can spend the time and effort to check their credit.

Here's a step-by-step break down of the critical steps:

1. Call possible tenants back and set appointments.

2. If possible, have more than one person at the same appointment.

3. Use the sign-in sheet to track advertising and highlight the need for an upfront option fee.

4. Let everyone walk around the house freely.

5. Hang out in the kitchen and at the end of their tour of the property ask if they would like to know how the Rent-to-Own Program works.

6. Use the flyer to outline the program, credits and buy out prices.

7. Don't get into too much detail – the information on the flyer is more than enough at this stage.

8. Transition from the flyer to an application by simply asking if they are interested in filling one out.

9. Move quickly to follow-up with the applications. Take a deposit right up front whenever possible. This shows commitment on the tenant's part.

10. Use a "Deposit Receipt" to hold the property.

Let's take a look at the Deposit Receipt form...

RECEIPT ONLY
DEPOSIT TO HOLD PROPERTY

_____ (Prospective Tenant) is agreeing to a deposit of $_____ paid to hold Prospective Tenant's position to rent-to-own the property located at:

_____

This deposit shall be paid as follows (outline how the option fee will be collected):

_____
_____
_____

ALL of Prospective Tenant's deposit will apply towards the purchase of said property (it will be considered as part of Prospective Tenant's Option Payment) provided Prospective Tenant lives up to all other terms of his/her/their agreements with Landlord. This deposit is nonrefundable, and Prospective Tenant must pay an additional $_____ option consideration by _____ and his/her/their first month's rent of $_____ before moving into the property on _____. If either of these payments is not received by Landlord on time then Landlord may at Landlord's sole discretion cancel agreement with Prospective Tenant and all money paid to Landlord by Prospective Tenant shall be kept as liquidated damages to cover application review, marketing costs to fill property, and lost opportunities. This agreement is subject to Landlord's final approval of Prospective Tenant's application. In the event that Landlord does not approve for any reason, Landlord may at his/her sole discretion refund all of Prospective Tenant's deposit and cancel this agreement. All option payments and first month's rent must be in the form of either certified funds or money order except at noted below.

Prospective Tenant understands that Prospective Tenant does NOT have a valid lease or option to purchase said property UNTIL Prospective Tenant makes both other payments described above on time and signs all further paperwork with Landlord, including Lease Agreement, Option to Purchase Agreement, Disclosure Forms, etc. In no case may the Prospective Tenant enter or otherwise occupy said property until ALL conditions and terms in this agreement have been fulfilled.

_____   _____
Prospective Tenant   Date

_____   _____
Landlord and/or Agent for Landlord   Date

If initial deposit is to be paid by cheque, initial next to this paragraph to show both parties understand and agree to the following: Tenant understands that he/she/they are making a nonrefundable deposit on this date to hold the property. Furthermore, Tenant hereby states that there are sufficient funds available to cover this check and that Tenant understands Landlord is relying upon the fact that this check will in fact clear. In the event this check does not clear for any reason, Tenant understands that Tenant shall be liable for prosecution and collection to the fullest extent of the law. Furthermore, Tenant understands that all remaining option money and first months' rent must be in the form of either certified funds or money order.

This is a form that you'll definitely want to have reviewed by a lawyer before you begin using it.

You'll notice that the deposit receipt form says the deposit is "non-refundable." There are exceptions to this:

If we are taking a deposit to hold the property and determine that their income isn't high enough, or that after the credit check there's something that doesn't meet our standards, we do refund the deposit.

Also, if we're taking multiple deposits on the property on the same day we'll scratch out "non-refundable" and write in "refundable."

We want the possible tenant to know that we're taking multiple deposits and when we review the applications we'll refund their deposit if we don't select them.

After we have reviewed their application, we'll call back and set a day and time to meet to complete the lease and option agreements.

At that point, we go through each point in both agreements in details.

<u>We go to extreme measures to be very clear and upfront with anyone signing a lease and option agreement with us.</u>

- For example, we explain that if they do not purchase the home that the option fee is lost.

- We also explain that the credits earned at no time can be used towards rent. They are only used towards purchasing the house.

We would rather lose someone at this stage in our relationship than have any confusion.

Some investors try to teach possible tenants every detail about rent-to-own programs during the tenant's first visit to the property.

Or worse, over the phone before the tenant has even seen the property.

That's like drinking from a firehouse.

Too much, too fast.

This is a process. A "system" that requires the proper steps to be performed in order to achieve the result.

Can you imagine someone's reaction who has never heard of Lease/Options or Rent-to-Own getting bombarded with details on appreciation rates used for buyout prices, and lease agreements and option fees and credits and handling repairs and paying for utilities?

We would run for the hills if someone laid all of that on us in one breath.

Take your time. Use the system we've covered here to do the heavy lifting for you.

We cannot emphasize this enough.

Want an easy way to check your progress?

Here's the best way to monitor yourself and self-correct.

We've done this enough that we know if:

> You get **12 leads** from your advertising.

➤ You should be able to get **<u>6 appointments</u>** for the property.

➤ And you should be able to get **<u>3 applications</u>** from those appointments.

This applies to all shapes and sizes of properties and all communities.

Chapter 23

How to Profit Big Time from
People Who Hate Your Property!

In this chapter, we're going to cover two of the most common questions we get around Lease/Options:

1. What to do with people who visit my property but tell me it's just not right for them?
2. And, what to do if your tenant does not exercise their option to buy the property?

People Who Hate Your Property

We accidentally stumbled onto the answer to the first question.

We both vividly recall situations where possible tenants told us that the property we were trying to rent out with a Lease/Option strategy was too small, or too dark, or had too much carpet, or had a series of other problems with it.

At first, we felt completely insulted.

And sometimes even embarrassed.

Especially if other tenants were looking around the property while someone was telling us how awful it was.

And remember, our properties are nice homes – so looking back we really had nothing to be embarrassed about.

But when we were first starting out with these, we really didn't know what to expect.

Now we understand that a certain percentage of people aren't going to like the property even if the walls were lined with gold!

Dealing with people's opinions is part of this business.

But then one day we actually chased someone down the driveway that looked around the property and quickly walked out.

And when we caught up to them we asked this magical question:

"If you don't like this property what is it that you're looking for?"

When they told us what they needed we then asked if we went off together and found such a home would they want to "rent-to-own" it from us.

Obviously, they did.

What was a negative situation a few minutes ago has now turned into a very positive situation.

This has a few big benefits:

1. We could buy another property knowing we had a tenant for it on Day 1. This gives you incredible peace of mind when buying an investment property. Before we

went "house shopping" we would collect a $1,000 refundable deposit that would be used towards the option fee. We used the "Deposit Receipt" form and just scratched out "non-refundable" and replaced it with "refundable." Then both of us would initial the change.

2. We still could focus on "good homes in good areas," so if the tenant wanted something that didn't fit our criteria we could steer them to something that did.

3. We always collect the entire "option fee" before we waive conditions on the new property purchase. This way we have thousands of dollars in hand before we even waived our conditions (usually for financing and inspection). This gives us peace of mind that the tenant is serious. We would often collect first and last month's rent the day we hand over the keys to them (we always ask for certified funds).

4. We have no vacancy period. As soon as we close on the property we have our tenant lined up ready to move in.

With all these benefits, people have asked us why we would ever buy a property without having the tenant for it first.

Here's the answer:

After spending thousands of dollars on real estate investing boot camps and courses, one of the main techniques taught to us was to do just that – get the tenant before the property.

The idea is that you advertise with little classified ads like this:

"Why rent when can you own?"

<u>Side Note</u>: If you spend any time on the rental section of Kijiji.ca you'll see ads like that. Most of these ads have no specific property they're advertising, just a generic ad, with a phone number.

You then try and meet up with some possible tenants to collect some form of deposit to show they are serious.

But we quickly learned that it was difficult to have people give us $5,000 or even $10,000 after meeting them for a few minutes in a Tim Hortons or Starbucks.

When possible tenants met us in one of our other properties first, they had a lot more trust in us.

We do know people who have found tenants before owning a property, but it's pretty rare. And you end up wasting a lot of time calling people back and trying to explain what "rent-to-own" is all about.

That's what happened to us. Because we didn't have a property to guide all the tenants to, we ended up sitting on the phone going through all the pros and cons of rent-to-own. It was very, very time consuming and the returns for our efforts were very low – basically zero!

So, it's possible; it's just not something we're fans of.

On the flip side, once you start owning a few properties and your name gets around that you're an investor who will buy properties, you'll have tenants calling you.

It's a beautiful thing!

What to do if your tenant doesn't buy the property?

There's a really easy answer for this:

You put out the "Rent-to-Own" sign on the lawn and start the process over again!

We know investors who actually prefer that the tenants do not buy the property because their "option fee" is non-refundable.

They can then re-rent the property and collect another option fee.

However, our goal is to always try and have the tenant buy the property. And we'll do everything we can to help them.

For example, after they move in and are settled (two to three months), we'll give them the name and number of our mortgage broker so that they can call and start putting a plan together to fix their credit.

Also, we'll remind them that the credits they are earning may not be enough to make up the entire down payment they'll need. And to start planning for that as well.

What are some reasons a tenant may not purchase?

1. We've had tenants get transferred with their jobs across the country. They would rather walk away than own a property in another province.

2. Some tenants get into relationships that break up and then they want out of the property. For example, we had one investor we work with collect $8,000 from a young couple. Three months later the boyfriend discovered that his pregnant girlfriend's baby was not his! She left

the home and he wanted to move to another city to get a fresh start. Unbelievable, but 100% true!

3. We've had some tenants who just didn't like the home after the lease was over. They obviously weren't interested in buying it.

4. We've had other tenants who outgrew the house and needed something bigger – so they didn't buy the property.

5. We've had some tenants lose their jobs and were no longer able to pay their bills.

This list could go on forever. You would be surprised at some of the situations that come up.

Here's the biggest piece of advice we can offer:

Always be upfront and honest. Before anyone moves into your Lease/Option property, make sure they understand the option fee is non-refundable.

If everyone is on the same page from Day 1 it makes things much easier if any issues arise.

One investor we work with has his tenants write out in their own handwriting that they understand the option fee is non-refundable.

That may sound a little extreme, but it definitely ensures everyone is on the same page.

What about if the tenant wants to buy out but needs more time?

If a tenant wants to buy the home but needs more time to save up for the down payment or needs another year to get their credit in good order, we'll offer several options:

1. We'll sign a new lease agreement for another year.

2. We'll also sign a brand-new option agreement for another year. We'll carry forward the existing credits and option fee.

3. Depending on the state of the market we'll either appreciate the home another 5% or leave the original buy out price. That's a case-by-case decision that is affected by market conditions at the time.

4. Lastly, we'll be flexible around the rental amount. If the tenants would rather have a lower rent for the next year, we'll offer that, but in return, we won't offer any more credits.

By doing this the tenants have time to get things in order.

The bottom line is by being flexible there's always a way to find something that will work for you and for the tenants. The key is to keep open lines of communication at all times.

One last thing … if you extend the lease multiple times be aware of the total amount of credits you are offering. You don't want to get into a situation where the tenant has tens of thousands of dollars in credits earned.

There are two reasons for this:

1. It may eat into your profits greatly if you haven't been appreciating the property every year.

2. The banks may not accept a buyer who has some huge amount of their down payment in "credits." We've never had a problem with this, but we're not interested in having a tenant with $50,000 in credits!

One last question we get about Lease/Options...

We're often asked how the purchase process works when the tenant wants to buy the property.

It's pretty straightforward:

1. You write up an offer to sell the home.

2. You use your Option Agreement to show proof that the option fee and credits were to be used towards the down payment of the purchase of the home. This is something your lawyer will ask for.

And on that note...

Lease/Options are definitely one of the more advanced investing options.

We recommend having everything reviewed by your lawyer before you get started.

We are not lawyers ourselves. Get a professional opinion before you begin.

Part 5:

Negotiation & Persuasion

Chapter 24

The Offer & Negotiation Tips

Let's jump into "The Offer Process."

We've covered a lot of stuff, and it's time we went over how you place an offer on a Property.

Using A Realtor Versus Going It Alone

Before we were licensed, we also made private offers on properties using offers we put together ourselves in Microsoft Word.

Although that's perfectly fine, we wouldn't recommend it.

If you're going to make a private offer, call a real estate lawyer, and they'll draft an offer up for you.

The last time we did that, they charged us $50.

Funny enough, they actually used the exact same form that Realtors use, the "Agreement of Purchase & Sale" but charged us to draft it up.

The standard agreement is made up of four pages and one extra page referred to as "Schedule A."

Schedule A is typically where you will list off the "conditions" of your offer. Typically, your offer will be conditional on obtaining financing and an inspection.

The first page is pretty self-explanatory. Here are the keys:

1. **Deposit:** You want this money to be held with your lawyer or a real estate brokerage. It's our preference not to have the deposit held with the seller's lawyer. Should the deal go bad on you it may be more difficult to get your deposit back than if you had it in a Brokerage's Trust account or your lawyer's account.

2. You must list off your **schedules** on Page 1 of the offer. If you ever, EVER, have anyone give you an offer with schedules to the offer that are not listed on page 1 it should raise alarm bells. They may not be listing Schedule A, B, C etc. because they're trying to hide it from someone (the bank, a lawyer etc.).

3. **Irrevocability:** That's the area where you put a date and time the seller has to accept your offer. In a hot market, sellers often ignore that because they're confident they'll get another offer. In a soft, slow market, you can really apply pressure to the seller by making then decide on your offer quickly. Typically, most offers allow for the seller to take 24hrs to make a decision.

4. **Completion Date** is the date the property will change possession. That's your "closing day."

Negotiation Tip: Even if you know the closing date the seller is looking for, and you can offer that to them, don't do it.

On your first offer, pick a day that you don't think the seller will want.

That way when you negotiate your offer, you have something else to give the seller other than just price.

Sometimes a closing day that matches what the seller needs is worth thousands of dollars to them.

Perhaps they can't move until their new house is ready, or the closing date of their next home is locked to a certain date and moving early would mean they have to rent somewhere for a month.

Don't underestimate the power of the Completion Date!

In a fast-moving, hot real estate market, this isn't as useful because sellers will just demand things. However, in a slow-moving real estate market, this little tip can save you thousands of dollars.

The key components of page 2 are…

1. **Chattels:** these are things that are not attached to the house physically but that you want to be included. For example, a stove, fridge, microwave, washer, dryer, all window coverings and blinds, all electric light fixtures, central air conditioning.

2. **Fixtures Excluded:** this may include things like a specific light fixture that the seller wants to keep or a set of silk curtains that they want to take with them.

3. **HST:** Make sure HST is listed as "included in" the Purchase Price. You don't want to be paying HST when you don't have to!

4. **Title Search:** This is usually set to 7 business days before closing. This allows the lawyers to search the

Title up to 7 days before closing to see if there are any problematic liens against the property. Perhaps the seller hasn't paid a contractor, and they placed a lien on the property. That will have to be settled before you can proceed.

Negotiation Tip: Ask for all the Chattels you can think of.

We've asked for things that aren't critical to us. Things like pianos or nice La-Z-Boy recliners or great kitchen tables.

That way when we go through the negotiation process we have extra things we can "give back" and negotiate with. This allows us to say things like, "Well, that kitchen table is really important to us, we need it because it fits that kitchen perfectly, but we can remove that if you are able to meet our price and closing date."

Each extra chattel that we have listed is one extra negotiating piece that we can use to our advantage. And perhaps you end up with some nice extras – we once ended up with a beautiful flat screen TV and a La-Z-Boy chair!

Page 3 of the Agreement of Purchase & Sale is very standard.

Page 4 of the offer is where both the buyer and seller sign off on their offer.

That is done on the top half of the page.

Now, there are two critical components
in the middle of this page:

1. **Spousal Consent:** This area must be signed if the home is a matrimonial home and one of the spouses is

not listed on Title. The other spouse must agree to sell the property, and that is done in this section.

2. **Confirmation of Acceptance:** Your offer may go back and forth multiple times while you are scratching out things like Price and Completion Date. Once you have agreed to an offer, it is accepted by signing in this section.

3. The **Acknowledgement** section at the bottom is for both parties to acknowledge that they have received signed copies of the offer.

Now, the only thing left is the Schedules. Typically, there is only one schedule used, Schedule A, that lists the critical conditions of our offer.

Pay very special attention to the wording of both the financing condition we use and the inspection condition.

You'll notice that both use the words "suitable to the Buyer."

This wording is important. It means that both the financing that we are able to obtain and the property inspection is "suitable" to us.

By using that type of wording, we can walk away from the Agreement if we don't like the interest rate or the way a property inspection looks.

We don't have to get into specifics about our decision.

Some realtors may get you to use clauses that allow the seller to make repairs to the property if anything should come up with the property during the inspection.

Also, some realtors may want you to put in writing the interest rate and mortgage amount you are seeking. That type of wording makes it harder for us to walk away from the deal.

Some other important notes and tips:

1. Allow at least 5 business days to obtain your financing. Even if you are pre-approved. Your bank can change their policies on a whim and we've seen pre-approvals become worthless once the bank sees the final offer. Always, always, give yourself time to finalize financing even if you are pre-approved. Also, ask your bank or mortgage broker for your mortgage commitment in writing.

2. You'll notice a small paragraph at the top of the schedule that states we'll pay the balance of the purchase price on the Completion Day. This is standard.

3. Also, in this example, we've included a clause to ask that the seller pays for our closing costs. Not all banks will accept this so even if you are able to negotiate it into your deal make sure you set aside money for closing costs. We've seen banks originally approve the deal, but then on the closing day have a change of heart. Be prepared! We cannot stress that enough.

Something you should know:

The bankers that approve your deal are referred to as underwriters. These underwriters come and go, just as people do in any role.

One underwriter may be fine with you asking for closing costs be paid by the seller but by the time your deal actually closes there may be a new underwriter in place that doesn't like that clause.

This is the real world, be prepared for every option.

Tip: We once had someone ask us to take our closing costs clause and put it on a separate schedule, Schedule B. That person then did not list Schedule B on the front page of the offer.

It became obvious to us that they were trying to hide this clause on another schedule and not show it to the banks.

We never, ever, operate that way.

You must handle yourself with honesty and integrity at all times.

Do things the proper way.

It will save you pain and grief in the long run.

We're all for pushing limits, but we do not believe in crossing the line.

Remember: Always get professional help with this stuff. At minimum, you need a qualified lawyer.

Chapter 25

The Science of Persuasion

Over the years it's become obvious to us that if you **really** want to achieve a high level of success at something, you'll have to dedicate hours to your craft.

In some circles, 1,000 hours is discussed as the time it takes to master anything, and in some recent new bestsellers, 10,000 hours is used.

Whatever it is, to really get good at something, you need to study and you need to practice.

With investing, of course, it's no different.

But what's often overlooked is the need to become a Jedi Master in not just "cash flow analysis" but you must develop other skills as well.

One skill that we initially overlooked was the ability to get people to "sign on the dotted line." Sales skills.

Even if you grew up in a family that treated salespeople as insects that needed to be exterminated, you'll eventually need to develop an appreciation for sales to maximize your efforts.

Real estate investing is a real business after all.

So with a vivid image of a crushed mosquito in mind, let's take a peek at some scientifically tested methods of improving your real estate investing.

We often hear that one of the most difficult things for investors to do is to get people to their rental property to view it and then sign a lease for it.

And obviously, mastering this skill can greatly increase your enjoyment of investing.

When you can fill a vacant room, house, apartment or condo with relative ease, your investing confidence begins to shoot through the roof.

And with confidences comes conviction and with conviction comes even greater and faster achievement.

With that, here are two things to consider when trying to fill your next property:

In Robert B. Cialdini's book, *Yes - 50 Scientifically Proven Ways to Be Persuasive*, he covers a strategy we've been using for some time.

Here's how it works...

If someone publicly states that they will act in a certain way, they are motivated to behave consistently with their commitment.

There's a study in the book where a restaurant owner reduced the percentage of no-shows for his dinner reservations by having his receptionist make a very subtle change to the way she took a reservation.

Instead of ending the call with, "Please call if you have to cancel."

She began saying, "Will you please call if you have to cancel?"

And as expected, nearly all customers committed to that question by verbally saying "yes."

The immediate results were impressive.

The restaurant no-show rate dropped from 30 percent to 10 percent.

That small change is enough to make or break an entire restaurant's success.

For years we've been doing the same thing with our showing appointments for properties.

After making the appointment with a possible tenant, we say, *"Will you please call if you have to cancel?"*

Just asking that question increased our appointment show rate at our properties.

And often we go one step further,

"Will you please call if you have to cancel because I won't make the long trip to the house if you can't make it? Will you do that?"

And of course 99% of the time we get a verbal "yes" from the person on the other end of the phone.

That adjustment has further increased our show rates to our properties.

Did you notice that in the above question we give a reason why we want them to call us if they're going to cancel?

That's by design.

In another one of Cialdini's books, he proves that by adding the word "because" to your request it increases acceptance and compliance with that request.

And he further proved that whatever is said after the word "because" makes no difference. It's the word "because" itself that increases acceptance of your request.

Neat, eh?

Now, because we're no slouches, let's take this one step further.

Cialdini ran another experiment.

College researchers asked volunteers to make verbal or written commitments to participate in a project.

And they got the same percentage of people to commit to the project whether it was verbal or written.

However, of those people who agreed to the project verbally, 17% actually showed up as promised.

Of the people who wrote down their intent to participate, 49% of those people kept their promise to show up.

Amazing.

People want to stay consistent with their actions. So, when they take the "action" of writing down their intent, it increases their commitment.

So how do we incorporate this knowledge into our investing?

Here's something we do ourselves fairly regularly, in addition to what we've discussed above...

We simply ask, *"Hey, do you have a pen and paper handy? I'll spell out the address of the property for you and give you my cell phone number."*

This way we get the possible tenant to make an "active" commitment to write down the address, our phone number, and usually our name and the time of appointment.

We can now almost accurately guess what our show rate will be at a property based on how successful we've been at getting people to take written action with us.

Let's recap:

To increase your show rate at your properties...

1. Get a verbal commitment from your possible tenants that they will call you if they have to cancel.

2. Give a reason why you're asking them for that by including the word "because" in your request.

3. Try to get the person to write down your phone number, the address of your property and even the time of the appointment if possible.

Don't force any of this stuff, you'll come across like a creep if you yell, "I'm not getting off the phone until you write down my phone number!"

Funny.

It's got to come out naturally.

And there you have it.

We have a bunch of other Jedi Mind Tricks up our sleeves ... but we'll save those for another chapter.

Part 6:

Advanced Lessons

Chapter 26

Property Management Tips
Learned the Hard Way

One of the most common questions we get is really focused around property management. It is:

Once you have the property, what are the top things that you should do to manage it properly?

There is no perfect guide to property management. Everyone has their own techniques that they use.

Normally, these are things they've done wrong for a period of time and have now figured out a way to fix their mistakes.

To answer this question, here are the top things that we do when managing one of our properties. And **yes**, these were all developed from our own missteps along the way.

We generally live and die by a set of rules we have, so we thought we'd share them with you.

The first rule is that you need to set expectations up front for any missed or late payments.

Often, we're really friendly when we are signing somebody up for a rental property, but during the explanation of the lease, we set a much firmer tone in that rent must be paid when it's due. We explain to them that if it's not paid by the second or third of the month, we'll notify them officially that rent is late and take official action at that point.

When we say that up front, there's no guessing when rent is late. In the past, we haven't really made that very clear, and it just works better when you're upfront about things. It can be an awkward thing to talk about -- especially when someone's first moving into the property. But just get it out of the way, you need to set expectations for missed or late payments.

> The second thing we do is put into the lease things like a garbage schedule, emergency contact numbers, email addresses, all that important information, in a bright red or yellow binder.

That way, when we hand it off to the tenants, they'll have all that information in the binder, and they won't forget it, especially if it's kind of an ugly colour! Then, if you need to call them or they have any questions about anything, you can just remind them that all the information they need (about the garbage schedule or about who to call for an emergency hot water tank replacement) is in that bright red or yellow binder.

Usually, people remember it if you refer to it like that. It helps them too because usually, people tend to scatter the paperwork the moment they get home, but this way we have seen people use it as a filing system as well.

This also relates back to setting expectations, because it positions you as more of an expert, not a newbie landlord.

We've seen some investors even do a walk around of the property, and go through the condition of the property with this binder so they can mark any repairs or anything already damaged, that way the tenant feels like you're protecting them because they won't get blamed for any of the damage.

Kind of like when you pick up a rental car and they walk you around the car looking for scratches before you leave.

Doing this shows you have a hold on the situation, and you're coming across as organized and professional as possible.

Another thing we have learned to do, to make our lives easier, is to put a lock box at our properties.

We mentioned in Part 3 that at one property, we used to get some calls because a particular tenant locked themselves out of their place a few times…and that turned into "many" times.

Driving out there to unlock the door was not on top of our list of things to do, so we just put out a lockbox (you get them at Home Depot, the kind realtors would use) and put an extra key for the front door inside. Then put it on the outside of the house, by attaching it to the garage.

That way, if they forget their key, you don't have to drive anywhere in the middle of the night. You can simply give them a lockbox code, and they can get the extra key. If this happens, you just flip down there the next day, or 2-3 days later, make sure the key is back in the lockbox and change the code, so no one else has access to it.

You always want to keep it locked down, so that they have to call to get access to it.

Huge tip and it saves lots of time!

And the added bonus is that it will even help you out sometimes.

For example, if you're going out to your property, the lockbox has the keys in it. So, you never have to think about ensuring you have the keys with you. You can pop in on any of your properties and get into anything you need. A lockbox is a really handy thing.

> Our next rule is invoicing for the monthly rent.

Most landlords just expect the monthly rent to show up. But you can actually send the little invoice via email.

When they get an invoice, it makes it seem really official. And if you're doing a lease option on the property, that's a perfect time to point out they earn a credit on the property. So, if you're giving them $200-$300 in credits every month on the property, you can summarize how many credits they've earned, which gives them the incentive to continue forward with the program, as they will see the credits growing every month.

This turns their invoice into a positive re-enforcer as well. It is something not a lot of people do, but a great thing to consider.

> Providing contact numbers where we can actually be reached is our next property management guideline.

We see a lot of people who become landlords for the first time, and they set up a phone number or email address they only check once a week.

You want to develop a relationship with your tenants. You want to give them a number that gets them in touch with you -- maybe not your home number or primary cell phone number, but you want to give them reassurance that you'll reach back out to them.

Quick Tip: Until you have a whole series of properties, you probably won't be using a property manager, so if you don't want to give your home number, set up a voicemail box that will email you the message (there are many services that do this - we use www.evoice.com).

You don't want to hide behind email addresses and phone numbers, that your tenants know you're only checking once in a blue moon. You really want to stay on top of the communication with your tenants, and it really goes a long way to developing the relationship and building a sense of trust, which will generally increase how they care for the property.

> You always, always, always want to do what you say you are going to do.

Often, we'll see people deal with tenants by promising the world.

They promise things like fixing up the garage or basement, but they never come through on it. It breaks the trust you have, and if you start breaking your word, they'll feel a little more inclined to break their word, which could mean not paying rent on time.

Whatever you say, make sure you do it because then you can hold them to whatever they say. It's a two-way street.

<u>We will also typically under-promise and over-deliver</u>.

For example, if you're ever doing renovations on a property, it can be tempting to tell them how glorious your renovations are going to be and all the halogen lights you're going to have. Great ceramics, stand up shower, etc.

We're guilty of this too! If the contractor comes in and you start going through cost over runs, you might cut back on those beautiful halogen lights you thought you were going to put in, but they've already had that upgrade set in their minds.

Now the upgrades you've done, while still being positive, are viewed as incomplete to your tenants because of the promises you made.

It's funny how this works, but it is true.

Keep your records organized.

As your real estate portfolio grows, it seems like paperwork starts to be everywhere.

Keep a copy of all your documents and your correspondence to your tenants for yourself (like the binder you're giving them) and make sure you have a filing system for your mortgage, lease, insurance documents. Keep it all handy -- you can either use a binder or a set of files for every property.

> Do things to keep the relationship on a good note.

Sometimes, you should swing by the property for positive reasons, not just negative reasons. If your tenants are paying the rent on time, it can be tempting to never go by the property.

If the only time you would normally go by is when they're paying their rent late, that can build a relationship with you where they're only really seeing you for bad reasons.

Instead, pop by every once in a while. In the summer, you can pop by and say hello. Make a point of going for no other reason than just to build the relationship -- it really goes far in running investment properties.

We normally drop off things at Christmas. This Christmas, it was Best Buy gift certificates, a bottle of wine, and some chocolates.

The last big point is that if you have late payments, you must act immediately.

> Do not get sucked into any drama!

Here's what we mean.

If someone's telling you they'll be paying you late, the natural next thing for them to do is give you an excuse as to why they're paying you late. You might be tempted to believe that reason, especially if they've been paying you up to date thus far.

If it happens once, it might be okay to accept it a few days late if they've paid on time for a good number of months straight. However, be very careful it only happens one time.

If they ever pay you late again, you must jump on things quickly. Otherwise what happens is that they think if they pay you late one month they can do it continuously.

Or even worse, they may say, "Hey, give me a break this month because (insert bad luck story here) and I'll pay you two month's rent, next month." If you accept that there is a very real chance that next month will come around they won't have paid you for the month they owe you, and they'll be short the current month.

So, now they are falling further and further behind.

They may say something like "I'll give you $500 then I'll give you another $500 in three weeks. I'll catch up by the end of this second month." Now you're going to be two months in, with no payments or partial payments.

You're now buying into their story. You may not get around to filing formal eviction notices or late payment notices until the beginning of the third month. If you buy into their story again, you're now a full three months in before you've done anything!

It can quickly spiral out of control.

It's so easy to ignore this tip, but we see it almost 90% of the time, especially with new landlords. You must stay on top of these things -- you can't buy into anyone's drama.

And not falling for the drama can be tough to do, especially when you are trying to build personal relationships with someone.

The way we do it is we usually say, "Look, we don't want to have to give you this, but it's really just to protect ourselves. According to this notice you have 10-14 days to true up, so we hope we don't get to that point, but we have to protect ourselves as well because this is a business for us."

We call it out and tell them what it is. It's the biggest point of property management we can tell you.

Every time you hear somebody share a story that it took six months for them to evict somebody out of a property it's usually because of the first 4-5 months they didn't do anything. Anyone who tells you it took them a long time to evict someone -- ask them what they did as soon as the person didn't pay the rent for the first time and you will probably get some insightful information.

The best property managers create systems for EVERYTHING they do. And that is exactly what you should set out to do.

That way, when a certain situation comes up, you just follow the guidelines for dealing with it.

There is no real right or wrong way to manage your properties. The key is to do what works for you and learn from the missteps along the way. Yes, unfortunately, there will be some lessons learned from experience.

We have never met a property manager or a landlord that did everything perfectly the first time around, and usually not the second either.

But that doesn't mean there can't be a first. Make it you, and let us know about it.

Chapter 27

Advanced Tips: Managing for
Maximum Cash Flow

We get a lot of the same questions asked by investors, so we're going to address them in this chapter. That way, you will have the answer handy when the time comes.

Question 1 - Can you talk a little bit more about how we connect with people when we're selling or renting a property?

This is a very important point, so let's go through this and make sure we're really clear.

When you're in a property, you <u>don't</u> want to turn it into a sales office.

What we do when someone comes to the door while we're speaking to somebody else at the property is run over to them immediately, shake their hand, and introduce ourselves.

The whole idea behind that is to make them feel comfortable and to welcome them to the property.

We never, ever, follow them around the house – ever!

We really dislike it when people follow us around a house when looking around the property. You feel trapped and that you can`t speak openly to the person you are with, and it doesn't allow your prospective tenant or buyer to get the "comfort of home" feeling that you want them to have.

You don't want to be on their backs.

Even if nobody else is there, we always tell them, "Take a look around. I'll just hang out in the kitchen."

As soon as you say that, there's a pressure that lifts off – they feel that it's okay to go roam around.

Showing Tip: Ensure all the lights inside the house are on before people arrive. This way you don`t have to follow them around to do it. This way you can just sit back and let them roam at their own pace.

The next goal of the showing is to start building trust with the potential client, and this doesn't matter whether you're renting, leasing, or selling the property (we look at buyers or tenants as clients to our real estate investment business).

After they've looked around the property, they will typically ask you a couple of questions about the place.

If they ask you a question you don't know the answer to, just admit you don't know the answer and that you'll follow up with them right away.

We find that if you use that strategy, it really builds trust because people have a pretty strong B.S. detector.

The key is to ensure that you follow-up with them the next day with the answer.

> When you want to quickly connect with somebody make sure the house doesn't seem like it's a used car lot.

While at your property, always keep everything casual and friendly.

Don't have pens and papers spread out all over the kitchen, and piles of paper you're referring to as "contracts."

A term like agreement is much less threatening to people.

Do any of us ever really want to sign a contract?

And be flexible with people. If they come to you to ask, "are these prices negotiable?" We'll always say, "Yeah. What works for you?"

If they suggest a price that's too low, we'll come back with, "Look, I'm willing to be flexible, but I can't go that low. I have to cover my costs too."

The goal is to never draw a line with people. Never tell someone that's the best offer, take it or leave it. Let people know you are flexible. It is best if they share with you what they're thinking.

Sometimes people will surprise you. They might have more money up front for the first few months of a property and then may want to reduce payments after that, and it might work out for you.

You never want to pressure people.

Also, find out what their interests are.

For example, if someone is in your property, find out why they're looking in that particular area and not just at that particular home.

If the house is close to where they work, the school their kids need, or public transit, you want to find out that information.

Then, when you're talking about the rent you can start positioning these points back to them as advantages to move into the property that don't have anything to do with the house.

Now, instead of pressuring people into signing rent based only on the house, you can try to use other things outside the house to your advantage. Help them realize this is a good deal, and it is where they want to live.

Whenever dealing with people, we always use an "apples to oranges" comparison.

For example: If prospective tenants know that a house down the street rented for $1,600 and we're asking $1,700, we'll never allow them to compare the houses straight up.

We'll do our homework, and we'll know that the house down the street might've had a slight difference. Maybe we have two full bathrooms, and that house had one and a half bathrooms or maybe it had a 30-year-old furnace in that house, and we have a mid or high-efficiency furnace in our house that will save them about $150 a month in the winter.

So, if we know some differences between the other properties in the area, when they start comparing rent in the area, they'll usually want to compare it as the same type of house, and we'll explain, "Hey look, you can't use that house as a comparison to this house. Here are the reasons why."

Question 2 – If we're looking at a rental property, what kind of mortgage rates and mortgage terms are we typically looking for?

Mortgage questions are tricky because the answers will change depending on your goals for the investment.

For example, we were in one of our properties this week and were reviewing the numbers on it. This place is on a 15-year amortized mortgage at a very good rate, which means that every month a chunk of the monthly mortgage payment is going toward principle. So, our mortgage is getting paid down faster than if we had a mortgage amortized over a longer period, maybe 20 or 25 years.

But our monthly payment to the bank is higher as well. So, every month that goes by, we make less monthly cash flow than we would if we had a longer amortization period.

Do you see how it can really differ depending on your goals?

Having said that, most investors (and we usually agree with this approach) extend the amortization period to 20-25 years.

They will end up paying more interest in the long run, but the interest portion of that monthly payment is tax deductible. That's a big advantage when owning investment real estate.

If you combine the tax advantages with the fact that your overall carrying costs are lower, it can be a good argument for the longer amortization.

So, instead of money being built up in the home, typically we prefer additional positive cash-flow every month that's going to go into our bank accounts.

It gives us the ability to reinvest that money into other investments.

> Cash flow is the key to investing, and it's the #1 principle when investing in real estate or any other investment. You want to try to invest for positive cash-flow.

Then when you get that cash-flow, you're free to use it as you wish.

So, we guess you could say we're fans of longer amortization periods in general.

Interest rates are an even more complex question.

Definitely, the best thing to do is sit down and figure out what your plan is for this property?

Is this a lease option property that you really think someone's going to be able to buy from you in 1-3 years?

If that's the case, maybe you go for a shorter-term mortgage or an open mortgage.

Or is this something you're looking at holding for the next 10-15 years?

If that's the case, you may want to lock in what your fixed costs are so that you have an understanding of what your cash-flow is.

There's something else to keep in mind, keep an eye on the current interest rate trends.

For example, if you feel that mortgage rates are either going to stay flat or drop a bit, it may be a good idea to go with a variable rate mortgage because the rates are generally lower.

But if you think that mortgage rates may be increasing over the next few years, it may be an opportunity lock in your mortgage a good fixed rate.

Historically, the variable rate mortgages have almost always saved people money over the term of the mortgage.

But if we hit times of high inflation, where interest rates are getting higher at a fairly quick pace, you might want to lock in.

The biggest thing you're going to want to do is sit down, work out the numbers, and look at what your plan is for this property.

Then choose the mortgage product based on that plan and how the numbers look for your specific investment.

Question 3 –When you're starting out investing, is it a good idea to do it yourself or should you use a realtor to either sell or rent your property?

We firmly believe that when you're starting out, the best thing you can do for a long-term investment career is to do it yourself at first.

This will help you grow as an investor. You'll gain sales, marketing and negotiation experience that will serve you well over the years.

When you do things yourself, whether renting or selling, you understand the advertising that happens with properties, the contracts and agreements that are involved, you get familiar with the negotiations that go back and forth, and you get familiar with the closing process if you're selling it, or accepting a new tenant and transferring the property over to the tenant.

Side note: When selling a property, you will get more marketing exposure when using a realtor to list it on the local MLS system. Be aware of that. If you choose to do that we would still recommend being involved in the entire process to learn the ropes.

After you've done it and you start to grow your portfolio, you might continue to do it yourself, or you may want to get other people to do it.

But now you know what is involved so you can set proper expectations with the people doing it for you.

For example, after you've rented three to four properties, you might want to lean on a property manager. By then you have the background and experience to know if they're really taking advantage of you and charging rates that are insane for small plumbing jobs, fixing a door handle, or changing a light fixture.

As for selling the property, once you've sold one, that's probably enough.

It'll give you enough experience to decide if you want to do another one yourself or use realtors.

We are licensed realtors, so this might sound a little strange, but we learned the most when we were doing things ourselves at first.

It gives you a real appreciation for the process.

Even if you try advertising for a couple weeks and talking with people, then putting a sign in the lawn and returning calls, it really increases your knowledge base.

> So, until you've done it a few times, either renting out or selling, there are real benefits to doing it yourself before you hand the job over to a professional.

Plus, some of the rates being charged (especially on property management) can be outrageous.

So, you really need to know what you're dealing with. Otherwise, you're going to lose a lot of your monthly cashflow!

Question 4 - "As far as everyday maintenance, those everyday tasks like shovelling the snow, cutting the grass, etc. - should those be outsourced?"

One of the valuable pieces of the investing puzzle you should have is a local handyman.

Very often you'll find free classified ads online, maybe a flyer in the grocery store, for a local handyman.

Or, one of the best sources for a local handyman is the closest used appliance store. Those stores typically service appliances and those service guys are usually great contacts for small jobs around your properties.

It's usually a retired guy, looking for the odd job to do. Those guys are gold!

If you find a good reliable handyman, they're awesome for some of the small issues you may face.

If you have a gate that's not closing right or a small plumbing leak, he's the guy to take care of it.

We had a loose tap once, on an older sink, which had individual taps -- one on the left-hand side, one on the right-hand side for hot and cold water.

One of these taps came loose, and we needed an old part we couldn't find, but our handyman knew where to get one.

He came in, was able to screw it on and it cost us $30. Someone like that can be really valuable.

It just goes back to building that team of people around you when you're investing in real estate.

When it comes to things like shovelling the snow and cutting the grass, we've had really good luck.

When it comes to grass cutting, we ask a neighbour on the street.

There's always someone on the street that just likes to sit on his porch or work on the garden, and just watch what other people are doing.

Those types of neighbours really like to be involved in the community, and know what's going on in the street.

And we've had really good experiences approaching people like that saying, "Would you be interested in just cutting our grass once or twice a week, or is there someone else that might be interested in doing something like that?"

We've never been let down, we've always been able to find someone, and it's nice because they take pride in the work they do, and they'll generally keep an eye on the place for you as well.

We've gone over to our rental properties before, and I've been told by the trusty neighbour, "Did you know they had a party last night?"

Sometimes, we get too much information, but it definitely comes in handy!

We like to always have someone like that on call for those types of things -- raking the leaves in the fall and so on.

When it comes to snow, what we put in our leases is that it is the tenant's responsibility to clear the walkway and shovel the snow.

In Ontario, even if that's in the lease, it's ultimately the landlord's responsibility.

You can put it in the lease and have them sign off on it, but when push comes to shove, it is the landlord's responsibility to have that cleared.

The same type of person who cuts your grass and takes care of the shrubs will likely be able to shovel your snow as well.

So, that person can be a handyman, or even more, a local neighbour.

I (Nick) learned quickly how valuable a person like that could be – with my first investment property. I was driving a Honda Civic.

A lawnmower doesn't fit into the trunk of a Honda Civic very well!

I realized quickly that I wanted someone else to be cutting the grass.

Bottom line: Professional lawn care and snow removal services are too expensive for a single property.

Find a local neighbour looking to make a few bucks! Make a flyer and drop it in the mailboxes on your street and you'll likely get a few calls right away.

Question 5 - "How much money would you take with an application if you were doing a lease option or a rent-to-own on a property?"

We've had multiple questions come in about how much money would we take from somebody as a deposit if we were doing a regular, straight-up rental.

Here's how we handle that.

If someone's coming to look at a rental property, whether a unit in a multi-unit building or a full single-family home rental or a single-family home with a lease option, you want enough money as a deposit so that they're not going to walk away.

Before, when we were starting out (like a lot of people), we would accept $100-$200 from somebody as enough money.

We then go and tell the other people that have been calling us, that the house was spoken for.

We then wait two days to sign leases and complete the deal, and the people would disappear.

We've then lost all momentum and have to start all over again.

It will crush you as a investor when that happens because you are on cloud nine when you start collecting money, then if the people walk away from it, you're heartbroken, and it's really hard to get the marketing in gear again.

What we do now is work with a magical number of $1,000.

If somebody gives us $1,000, it's unlikely they'll walk away.

They're pretty serious, and the deposit form we use for the property states that it's non-refundable.

We take a deposit on this property, non-refundable, and we'll either put it toward last month's rent or toward the option money on the property if we're doing a lease option on the property.

$1,000 is the minimum amount we'll accept.

Only one time, we've had it happen where somebody actually did walk away from $1,000 -- if you can believe it!

It was a non-refundable deposit on a lease option property that somebody gave $1,000 for, and they walked away.

But it has only happened once.

We've had other amounts walked away from $50, $200 has been pretty common, but as soon as you get to $1,000, it's very rare someone is going to walk away from that, they're usually very serious.

Never take a $1,000 personal cheque and start telling other people that the property is spoken for -- make sure that cheque is cashed first.

A lot of people don't know this, but in Canada, if a cheque is written on the Bank of Nova Scotia or Bank of Montreal, you can take the cheque to that bank, and get it certified.

You can pay $14 to have it certified, so you know that money is there when you go to deposit it into your bank.

$1,000 is definitely a magical number.

Also, we'll never hand over the keys until we have all the money we're expecting.

But as a deposit on a rental property, at a minimum of $1,000, we set a really quick agenda and schedule as to when we're going to pick up the rest of the money.

We don't sit on $1,000 for six weeks if they're going to take eight weeks to move in.

If they're going to take eight weeks to move into the property because they have to give 60-days' notice elsewhere, we'll take $1,000 then we'll tell them "Okay, in two weeks we'll need money from you, and then in another two weeks, we need more money," because if you take $1,000 and then sit on your property vacant for two months that's not going to cover your expenses.

If they walk away, you're going to be left holding the bag.

Even if they're going to take a full two months to move in, set a really quick schedule to be collecting more money before the move in date.

But overall, $1,000 is the magical number to accept as a deposit for a rental property.

Question 6 - "If you have a rental property or looking to do rent-to-own on a property, what do you think about a third-party placement agency to rent out the home?"

With a typical rental, it may not be a bad idea, as long as you can find a reputable firm.

Sometimes, there's not as much desire for this agency or company to rent out your home as there is for you to rent out your own home.

We strongly believe when you're investing in real estate, you should go through the process at least one time yourself.

How do you know that this company will or won't to do a good job if you have nothing to compare it to and no first-hand experience?

That's a big point.

Unless you do it yourself, you don't know if anyone is doing a good job for you or a bad job.

By handling your own property, it really makes you grow as a person and as an investor.

If this agency fills your home and those people move out at three months, now you have to use an agency to fill your home again, and you're going to have to pay them again to do it.

There's no incentive for them to get a long-term tenant.

Being able to do it yourself is great so that if you need to step in, you can. It's a powerful thing.

There's one investor that had an investment property, it was supposed to be a hands-off investment property, and the tenant was provided with property management included.

The investor wasn't supposed to do a thing. He was in a rental pool, and his property went negative cash flow pretty quickly. Because the property management company let a few people move out and they weren't filling the property, there wasn't enough income coming in to pay the mortgage.

He had never done this himself, so now he was forced to learn about it quickly, but he couldn't see the warning signs that this was coming because he had no experience running a property.

Yes, you can definitely use a company if you're able to find a reputable one, but we would strongly suggest for anyone to do it themselves the first time.

That's our advice for a typical rental.

When it comes to a rent-to-own or lease option, there are very few people that are going to understand the process and be able to strive for a good down payment, higher monthly rent and lock in those good numbers for you.

If it's a lease option, again, especially the first time, you want to go through the process yourself.

We haven't been able to find a good company to fill homes with lease options.

If anyone knows of one, feel free to send it over to us, but they're hard to come by.

Yes, you can use placement agencies, but if you want to become a real investor, you've got to do a little bit of the work yourself.

Especially as you are initially growing your portfolio.

Question 7 - "I'm not averse to occasional busy times that this investment requires, and I understand there is some work to be done. I have common sense, home ownership experience and even owned a student rental property. I do my own painting and landscaping. But we're busy with teen and pre-teen kids. Do we have a shot at this?"

This last question is a really good question, and it's probably one that you have thought yourself.

We only got it from one person, but we're sure it's something going through a lot of peoples' minds -- it's really just about the possibilities of making this happen.

The short answer is yes, absolutely.

Why can we say that with such confidence?

Because we've worked with thousands of investors over the last decade, and we've seen them all become successful.

They come from every different area of life, with different backgrounds, ethnicities, professions, all sorts of stuff.

The success isn't limited to anyone really, and most of the people that we've worked with (ourselves included) are really not the handiest people.

We can do little stuff, but when it comes to hard labour, electrical work, drywall, plumbing...those are not our strengths at all, and we have no idea what we're doing.

For most of the stuff now, we pretty much hire someone to do everything, but you don't need to be a renovation specialist to get into real estate investing.

We think from all the stuff we see on TV, and that we read about, it's probably one of the biggest misconceptions about real estate investing.

If you get into the right property in the right area, you can start making positive cash flow and a good income real estate investing with doing little or no work whatsoever, and that includes cleaning the property.

There have been many properties that we've purchased and seen the homeowners leave them in great shape, so we haven't had to do a single thing except show it to people.

So, absolutely you can do it, we think the biggest challenge in anyone looking to invest whether for the first time or not is there is always a certain amount of fear.

We still second-guess the numbers every time we look at a property before we're going to sign the documents.

We will look at the spreadsheets, and a number of times, over and over to make sure we have an understanding of it.

Are the numbers right, are we missing anything, do we have everything straight? It's natural to feel that way.

Especially with your first one, there's going to be more of that, but that's where it comes down to really getting a team around you that can help you succeed.

You can look at other successful investors and see what they've done or find some experts to help you through the process.

We're here to help you through the process as well, so you can leverage us and the people we work with to go through that as well.

You absolutely have a shot at this.

We remember two young sisters jumping in on a property by themselves with no other support from their family and they had never touched a hammer or screwdriver in their lives.

Friends getting together to do it, spouses doing it if you have a supportive spouse, fantastic.

And it almost seems like the people that are kind of new to it pull it off the best, because they follow up with things and they don't take anything for granted.

People who've had a lot of experience in things sometimes assume they know everything and trip themselves up.

So, young and old, by yourself or with teams of people, we've seen it all.

You can do it and you will.

Chapter 28

Housing Market Fundamentals

Way back in Part 1 of this book, we talked about a lot of the fundamentals that we look for when we're looking at properties.

When we're looking at specific areas for the type of properties that typically make good investments, we consider things like immigration or migration. That means we're looking for people who are moving into the area, which will increase the demand for housing.

We're also looking at new transportation routes, job diversification within the area, new employers setting up shop, along with the employment or unemployment levels of the area. So, we're looking at those fundamentals as well as few others.

But one thing that we haven't discussed is the need to look at the real estate market as a whole.

As investors, we need to start understanding what the real estate market as a whole is doing so we can look at some trends and patterns and play those to our advantage.

It's kind of like we are taking an economist's point of view.

A good example is to look at house prices and what they're doing.

For example, consider what had happened from 2006 to 2009 in the US housing market. If you were looking at those trends, there was a massive downswing. As an investor, you want to understand some insights into that downswing, so that you can adjust your portfolio and your investment strategy accordingly.

In Canada, we never really got hit with that severe downturn, and there are some key reasons why we didn't. But let's just look at the market as a whole for a second.

The first thing that you should know is <u>the biggest thing that drives housing markets or a sustainable housing price increase is affordability</u>.

With affordability, we are looking at the average income of a family in a specific area (community, city, province), or an average homeowner.

So, if wages are increasing in a city, then the house prices can sustainably increase as well because the affordability hasn't really changed.

For example, when someone is looking to buy a house, they can only spend so much of their income on that home without getting themselves into financial difficulty (because they have other expenses as well; things like cars, and groceries, kids, clothes, utility payments, etc.).

They can't very well spend all their money on a mortgage payment, right?

Reasonably, they're looking at spending about 40% of their income on shelter. That means they can only afford home prices that don't take up more income than that.

So, if the average person looking for a house is making $50,000 per year of income, and let's say we are taking 40% of that for housing, they can spend about $20,000 of that income on mortgage payments. So, that works out to about $1,650 a month.

If wages were to go up, perhaps in this example they moved from $50,000 to $60,000, then the amount of money that can be spent on a typical mortgage can increase as well. Because people can still afford to spend about 40% or about $2,000 per month and have extra money left over for all the other expenses that you have to worry about.

The wage increase changes the amount of demand in the housing market because it creates more affordability.

As wages increase, more people can afford the average home which can cause prices to start rising.

For example, let's pretend we are investing in an area where the average home price is $400,000, and to be able to afford that home you need to be making at least $50,000 per year.

There are a limited number of people that make that amount of money and can afford that price of home in any given area. As wages rise, more people will be able to buy that house.

Because not only can everyone that was making $50,000 still afford the home, now people that were making less than $50,000 can afford the home because their salaries have gone up to the point where they can afford it.

As more people that can afford homes at a certain price point enter the housing market, demand picks up causing home prices to rise.

It is simple supply and demand. If the supply of homes at a price point stays the same and there are more buyers, prices go up.

Think about what would happen if the grocery store only got one bag of milk a day. How much could they charge?

Now let's take a quick look at what happens when home prices start moving upwards, and wages don't increase (they stay at $50,000).

If we look at the same $400,000 home and home prices start to creep up by 10%, the same home now costs $440,000. It changes the market because wages haven't kept up, and now not as many people can afford the home, and the demand for that home will slowly drop because there are fewer people in the market who can afford it.

It's all related to supply and demand. The demand is the number of people that can now afford that house because of the price increases.

The number one thing to realize about real estate markets is that housing affordability is the biggest factor that drives sustainable increases.

A sustainable price increase is one that has some foundation underneath it. It isn't a speculation bubble where everyone is lining up at a new home sales offices because it is the next "great" development.

Sustainable price increases are less likely to be wiped out when the market fluctuates because there are real economic reasons that justify the price.

OK, let's move on to two of the biggest factors that can cause real estate price fluctuations.

Those are interest rates and inflation, and they really go hand in hand.

The government likes to have a bit of inflation in the economy for a variety of reasons (which we need to save for another day).

One of the impacts of inflation is a rise in the cost of goods. That is why a chocolate bar that used to cost $0.25 now costs $1.75.

But it doesn't just apply to chocolate; it applies to all the stuff that we need to build a house as well. Over time, the cost of goods to build homes generally goes up.

Example: The cost of wood to make the frame, steel to make the nails, oil to make asphalt shingles for the roof, etc. rise over time.

As materials and labour prices go up to build a home, naturally, there are price increases.

Natural price increases caused by normal levels of inflation are generally okay because normally wages are going up at the same time and at about the same rate.

Things start to get overheated when you see large percentage (double digit) price increases in homes from one year to the next. Sometimes it may be because a lot of people are moving into the area or maybe it's just an overheated, overhyped economy.

A really good example of this happened from roughly 2005 to about 2008 in Western Canada. There was a huge, huge, up-swing in real estate prices.

In Alberta, there was a lot of money being put into oil sands projects because of the increased price of oil. The price increase made it more feasible for companies to go and get oil out of the tar sands in Alberta.

This caused more and more people to move into that area because the oil companies were able to pay good wages. These wages led to a big increase in the affordability of the homes in Alberta.

All these new oil jobs caused wages to jump, which led to a big increase in the demand for homes from people that had lived there for a long time and from the new people that were moving in for the new jobs. It resulted in a big spike in demand for homes.

And because of the increasing demand, the price of homes kept rising too.

So, if in the past a house went on the market, there may have been five people who liked it and could afford it. But now you had those 5 people plus other locals who now had these new, better-paying jobs, and even more people who were moving into the area, for the new jobs, that needed a house.

Now you have fifteen people who like that house and who can afford it. They all throw in offers, which drive the price of that home up, subsequently driving up the price of the house down the street.

The overall affordability had increased because people could afford more with the money they were making. This resulted in a super-fast ramp-up in real estate prices. But anything that goes up so high, so quickly isn't sustainable.

It went up so fast that real estate prices swung past the point of affordability. Buyers kept pushing the limits to see how much home they could afford, and sellers kept asking for more and more to see how much they could get.

But eventually, oil prices came back down to Earth and oil companies said, "Hey, let's slow down and stop bringing all these people into the area. Let's stop hiring more and more people for these high wages." Then, all of the sudden, you had fewer people who could afford to pay that top dollar for the house and prices came back down to be more in line with affordability.

That is how changing material and labour costs or inflation can cause real estate market changes.

This is where interest rates come into the equation.

More things than you probably ever want to know about affect interest rates. For our purposes, we are going to take a very high-level look at them. The key thing that we need to watch for is the mortgage rates that are offered by the banks.

They have a big impact on the price a buyer can afford to pay for a home, which can cause interest rates to cause general trends in housing prices to change as well.

Side Note: While we discuss these market changes, we should keep in mind earlier chapters. We look for properties in areas with strong fundamentals to reduce the impact that these other factors, we are currently discussing, have on the specific markets we own property in.

Fluctuations are easier to handle when you're in a good community that has a lot of different things going for it (strong fundamentals).

When the housing market (prices) starts to increase too fast the government steps in and says, *"Whoa, hold on here. We feel that if prices are increasing so fast, that we're creating an overheated real estate market."*

Maybe they're going up too fast, and wages aren't keeping up with it. Perhaps interest rates are so low it is causing a big increase in affordability because people are borrowing all this cheap money.

Remember, the goal is sustainable growth.

If things move too fast, it isn't sustainable, so the government wants to regulate it.

One way they do this is by raising interest rates. When they raise interest rates, it makes it more expensive for us to have mortgages. It's pretty simple, right?

When interest rates rise from 5% to 6% on a $400,000 mortgage, amortized over 25 years, the monthly payment will increase by approximately $233.

That $233 change starts to reduce the number of people that can afford homes of that level, which slows demand, and slows or eliminates price increases.

It's that simple.

In markets that have gone up too fast, it can cause a price correction, but most often it is only a fraction of the overall price increases that real estate market saw during the run-up in prices.

For example, in the Alberta scenario, prices fell from their peaks, but overall, they were much higher than before the new jobs, and higher incomes caused them to start rising.

Interest rate moves are the government's way of trying to regulate the overall market, so things don't get out of hand.

If they see that the economy is very, very slow and that the housing market is not really moving, they will bring interest rates right down. Then, suddenly, it becomes cheaper to borrow money, and then more people can afford the average home, and it makes the housing market more active, right?

Right!

As investors, what we want to understand is that when we see those interest rate fluctuations, the reason it changes the housing market isn't just because interest rates change, it is because it changes the affordability of the house.

We could get into all sorts of overly detailed economic numbers and indicators to analyze the housing market but keeping it simple is often the best approach.

Now that you know this, it will help you gauge current and future investments by understanding what the overall market picture is, and planning your cash flow and number crunching around it.

Chapter 29

Using Joint Venture Agreements to Purchase Cash Flowing Real Estate

Why Would You Consider a Joint Venture?

The most common reason people consider a Joint Venture relationship is to overcome either:

A) A lack of capital.

B) A lack of experience.

Let's look at lack of capital first...

During your investment career, you'll likely come across a point in time (sooner than later) where you'll know of a great opportunity to invest, but you won't have access to the capital to acquire the asset.

Either because your capital is tied up in the form of equity in some of your properties.

Or, because you've simply run out of cash buying properties.

Raising more investment capital is the #1 business challenge across every single business ever created!

So, if you find yourself in this position, don't feel alone! It's a common hurdle.

One creative way to get around this little problem is to Joint Venture with someone who does have the capital to invest.

A very common scenario in smaller residential real estate investments, let's says 6 units or less, is this:

Partner A: Puts up the capital for the down payment of the investment.

Partner B: Puts in the work required to manage or fix-up and sell the investment.

Partner A and Partner B split the proceeds of cash flow and equity build-up 50/50.

Notice that in this scenario each partner has something to offer the other.

Partner A has the cash.

And Partner B has the skills and experience to manage or fix-up and sell the property.

It's an exchange of value.

Often, beginner investors want to form Joint Ventures because they have zero cash and zero experience.

In that scenario, you offer very little to a potential Joint Venture partner.

It's the classic catch 22.

If you find yourself in such a position, you'll need to either save up some cash for your own down payment even if that means it takes longer for you to start investing.

OR...

Offer to manage a property for free to an investor to gain experience.

Keep in mind that you'll have to prove to the investor that you're detail oriented, have a car to get around, can negotiate with people, are willing to take calls at all hours, etc.

Let's look at the next reason to Joint Venture...lack of experience...

Another reason many investors with sufficient cash to invest alone choose to invest with Joint Ventures is their lack of experience.

If you've never purchased and managed a 26-Unit apartment building, you may not want to jump in all alone.

That size of building likely has a fair amount of landscaping to deal with, parking to keep organized, common areas, like stairwells and hallways to keep clean, garbage to take out, vacancies to deal with, evictions to handle, etc.

And it's not large enough to warrant or even afford a full-time property manager.

These types of building have a "Super" who is typically one of the tenants in the building that manages a lot of this stuff for you in exchange for a discount on their rent.

If rent is perhaps $900 per month then the Super is likely

only paying $300 or so.

But even with a Super, you'll likely be much better off Joint Venturing with someone with experience in this type of property.

If you can find someone with a proven track record that can keep vacancies low and cash flow high, it may be a fair exchange of value to give up some portion of the cash flow and equity build-up to gain their expertise and have them manage the day-to-day activities of the investment.

What About Buy-Fix-Sell?

If you're purchasing a property to "fix it up and sell it for a profit" then perhaps you're looking for someone to partner with that is a contractor.

You put up the money, and they do all the work.

You split the profits at an agreed upon rate.

Of Course, There Is One More Form of Joint Venture...

There are situations where two partners put up the same amount of capital and share in the duties of the investment.

And there's nothing wrong with this either.

We see many beginners choosing this path.

Often with two, three, even ten or more partners.

Just remember that with the more partners the more complex decision making can get.

Ultimately, the combinations of partners, ownership

percentages and responsibility division are endless. You can get as creative as you'd like.

Using Joint Venture Agreements

Out of all the reasons to Joint Venture with someone the most successful that we've seen have been...

Where each partner's role has been clearly defined in an official Joint Venture Agreement.

Verbal agreements or agreements where everyone has a "vague understanding" of their role get messy quickly.

Before entering into any type of Joint Venture agreement you should:

1. **Have your lawyer review the agreement!**

   Each Province and Territory in Canada will have slight differences on how they legally deal with these – have the agreement reviewed by your lawyer before signing it.

   This is mandatory, and it's for own protection.

2. **Get expert advice on the investment.** Just because someone is about to take your money and put it into a "slam dunk" investment in Costa Rica, doesn't actually mean you'll make any money.

   Have someone review the deal you are about to sign before you proceed.

   We have found that accountants who have at least 20 years of experience under their belts are very good resources for this. They've pretty much seen almost every sort of failed business relationship by that time and can offer good advice.

But remember, accountants are by nature risk-averse. So, don't let them talk you out of a deal because they don't have experience with it.

You want to find someone who has had experience with the type of Joint Venture you're putting together to offer you advice.

We had an accountant once talk us out of something because of his own fear of the project. We found out later that the investment was very sound and the cash flow projections were actually very conservative.

<u>Bottom Line</u>: Get specific advice from someone with experience in the exact type of investment you are considering.

3. **Get to know your Joint Venture partner.** How well do you know them? Remember, everyone is friends when the deal begins, but at the first sign of trouble, things can change.

Let's put it to you this way…

How will your partner react when they either have to put in more work into the project than they initially believed?

Or, have to put in much more money into the project than initially budgeted?

We rarely see investments go perfectly according to plan.

When someone has to cough up an extra $20,000 for

an unforeseen delay or repair, how will they react?

How financially strong is the Joint Venture relationship?

Does the partnership have enough money available to fund delays, cost overages, unforeseen events, and changes in interest rates, changes in the market?

Plan for the worst case and budget accordingly.

Have these conversations up front and put them in writing!

Chapter 30

Getting a Big Fat Cheque from Your Real Estate Investments

There are two points we want to drive home in this final chapter:

Action and Exit Plans

- Can you imagine a surgeon deciding to "wing it" when performing a heart operation instead of applying what they've learned?

- Or a financial advisor drawing names out of a hat to determine the stocks she's recommending to her clients instead of applying what she's learned?

- Or a University graduate putting his degree in a drawer somewhere and sitting on the couch for the rest of his days doing nothing with his education?

Amazingly, these things happen every single day.

People get training. They get inspired.

But they simply toss them both away like yesterday's garbage. They simply decide not to use the resources they've gathered (and likely paid for).

Please, don't let this happen to you.

Don't look back with regret on more wasted money and time.

Instead, make a decision right here to put everything you've learned to good use. Whatever motivation you need to draw on, go and do it. Now. You owe it to yourself.

Listen, one of our first jobs was making $3.50/hour in a convenience store. $3.50 per hour! We then worked picking up garbage and cleaning out toilets on construction sites. As teenagers, our family split up over hundreds of thousands of dollars in losses in real estate losses (the family has since reunited!).

One of our first properties was negative cash flow and needed tens of thousands of dollars in repairs shortly after buying it. It had the oldest and dirtiest shag floors you've ever seen.

We couldn't fill vacancies quickly or efficiently.

Another property had so much dirty tar on the windows that you couldn't see the sunlight outside and had three different basement leaks in the first 12 months.

We could have easily quit at any of these things.

But we didn't.

We would not quit without a fight.

And those rough properties have turned into shiny diamonds.

We have become stronger because we didn't give up.

And we're here today to urge you to do the same.

We're not cheerleaders, and you don't want to see us sing or wear short skirts! But we're here to tell you that you can do this.

You absolutely can.

We can't make you.

But we can hold up a mirror to your face and say, "Hey, look in the mirror, what are YOU going to do here?"

When you come to the end of your life, will you have regrets or will you go for it?

We'll leave you with this anonymous quote…

"Life should NOT be a journey to the grave with the intention of arriving safely in an attractive and well-preserved body, but rather to skid in sideways, chocolate in one hand, champagne in the other, body thoroughly used up, totally worn out and screaming, 'WOO HOO what a ride!'"

OK, cheerleading over.

Let's talk exit plans…

To get a **big fat cheque** from your properties you need to keep two things in mind:

1. What is the exit plan for this particular property?

2. Am I using the proper time frame to make my decisions?

We believe it's Warren Buffet who said, *"You shouldn't own anything for ten minutes that you wouldn't own for 10 years."*

And we couldn't agree more.

One of the most common mistakes we see investors make is getting caught up in the excitement of the "deal" that they make emotional decisions.

For example…

Just the other day we had someone here in Canada comment to us that they can't believe we had not bought anything in Florida during the housing crash there in 2009.

Just because you could buy a nice property in a gated community for $120,000 when it was worth $240,000 18 months earlier, it doesn't mean it's a good deal for us.

Why?

Because we don't have a clear exit plan.

Even though we may be able to produce positive cash flow on that Florida property, we don't have a clear exit plan.

What happens if the other condos don't get sold in that community? What happens to the condo fees, what happens to the community?

Can we sell the property quickly if we need to?

Unless we can get those answers, we stay away.

If we needed to sell that property for some unknown reason, we can't see what the exit plan would be.

Many successful investors have lost everything on a single property that they couldn't get rid of quickly enough.

Ask us how we know.

Here's another example...

Here in Canada, there are many "deals" floating around. Whether it's a vacation property in Whistler or a condo in Vancouver or a townhome in Toronto.

There's plenty of opportunity.

However, often we see investors get caught up in the numbers.

For example, if you could pick up a Lease/Option property that produces $1,000 a month, would you be interested?

Of course, right?

But what if we told you the property is a higher end home in a small community.

How will you get a new tenant in such a property if your first tenant leaves you?

Does such a small community have a large number of people will to pay the $3,000/month rent that you originally obtained?

Likely not.

And can you sell the property quickly if you need to, even if the real estate market freezes up because of high-interest rates?

Likely not.

Some Properties Don't Need Exit Plans

What do we mean?

Well, sometimes you'll have a property like a student rental property.

That type of property is harder to sell because the financing for it requires a down payment of 25% to 30% in most cases.

And it's trickier to refinance for the same reasons. You can't refinance it up to 90% of its value, and many banks won't want to refinance it at all.

You need to be aware of that.

But with that type of property perhaps the exit plan is hanging on to it and making it a permanent part of your legacy.

An asset that will be part of the family for many years.

And when it's fully paid off your family can sell it for a bit of a discount or by holding back a second mortgage if they need to.

They'll have options because there's tons of equity in it.

If you go into that type of investment thinking long-term about your exit plan, you'll be prepared for anything.

However, if you go into a student rental looking to hold it for 12 to 36 months and then selling it for a profit, you may be in for a shock.

Real estate cycles often last for years.

When the time comes to sell your student rental property, and you find yourself in a down real estate market you then have:

1. A property that's slightly harder to sell because of the down payment requirements.

2. A property that has very little equity in it so you can't price it aggressively without possibly losing money when you sell it.

3. A property that becomes a source of frustration instead of inspiration.

There's a lot of money to be made in real estate.

And to get that big fat cheque, whether it's monthly cash flow or profit on a sale, you must think about exit plans.

Never be blinded by a great deal.

A property is often a great deal for a reason.

And if you can't find out what that reason is, stay away.

We're not trying to scare you here.

We like you so much and care for your success so much that we want to prepare you for as much as possible.

Over the years, going as far back as you can get data, real estate has always been and will continue to be an amazing investment vehicle.

You have at your fingertips the opportunity of a lifetime.

You live in a great country, with a great financial system, with secure laws and ethics.

Chapter 30's Assignment

Determine your exit plans. For any properties you already own, map out an exit strategy for them. For properties that you are currently looking at acquiring don't purchase them until you have a very clear exit plan for it … whether it's selling it, keeping it, refinancing it, whatever it is, map it out. Make some decisions today and take some initial steps that will position you for a big paycheque.

Next Steps...

So, you're probably wondering what comes next?

1. Check out our podcast, *The Your Life! Your Terms! Show* where we talk real estate, business building, the economy, nutrition, fitness and anything else to help us all live life on our own terms. Subscribe and  listen at www.RockStarInnerCircle.com/podcast.

2. You can also find all of our videos and articles on our blog by visiting www.RockStarInnerCircle.com/blog.

3. We hope you enjoyed this book. It covered a lot, yet there's always more to share. That's why we're offering you a free digital copy of *Income for Life for Canadians* at www.FreeCanadianBook.com.

In this book you'll learn how one property can give you five different income streams, trends to be aware of when investing, how to turn one property into multiple without any of your own money, and much more!

4. We also hold a live Free Training Class in our offices where we share the exact strategies we're using today with Canadian investors. You can grab your seat by visiting: www.CanadianRealEstateTraining.com.

In this class you'll learn:

- The step-by-step process for finding the best income properties in the GTA and Golden Horseshoe.

- The latest Canadian mortgage and financing options available to investors.

- The different strategies we're using in today's market to produce positive monthly cash flow.

- Examples and current case studies of other investor's who have recently taken action so that you can learn the latest "from the streets."

This class regularly fills to capacity and we have limiting seating in our training room, so don't wait to grab your seat.

You can register right here:

www.CanadianRealEstateTraining.com

We'd love to see you at our next class.

In the meantime, we're not saying "good-bye." We're just saying, "We'll see you later!"

Made in the USA
Monee, IL
25 April 2021